101 STRATEGIES TO CONNECT, INFLUENCE, AND INSPIRE

SPEAK WITH IMPACT

M DAVID RAJ - M SQUARE MOTIVATIONS

To all the leaders, communicators, and dreamers who strive to make a
meaningful impact.

May these pages empower you to speak with clarity, connect with purpose,
and inspire with passion. Your voice has the power to shape the world.
Never underestimate it.

This book is for you—dedicated to those who are ready to lead with heart
and leave a lasting impression.

Contents

Foreword   *xi*

Preface   *xiii*

Acknowledgements   *xv*

Prologue   *xvii*

"Ways To Connect" Focus On Building Relationships, Trust, And Rapport

1. Smile- It's Your First Connection Tool   3

2. Use The Person's Name In Conversations- It Shows You Value Them   9

3. Active Listening- Listen To Understand, Not Just Reply   14

4. Maintain Eye Contact- It Creates Trust   19

5. Mirror Their Body Language- It Builds Rapport   24

6. Find Common Ground In Conversations- Start With Shared Interests   30

7. Compliment Genuinely- It Opens Hearts   38

8. Use Open Body Language- Crossed Arms Can Close The Connection   42

9. Send Handwritten Notes Of Appreciation- It's A Personal Touch   46

10. Follow Up After Meetings- It Strengthens The Relationship   50

11. Remember Important Dates—it Shows You Care   53

12. Practice Gratitude Often—it Deepens Bonds   55

13. Share A Laugh—it Builds A Sense Of Camaraderie   58

14. Be Punctual—it Shows Respect For Others' Time   60

15. Stay Curious—ask Thoughtful Questions To Show Interest   62

16. Offer Help Without Being Asked—it Builds Goodwill   64

17. Respect Cultural Differences—it Demonstrates Understanding   66

18. Share Your Authentic Self—it Fosters Trust   68

19. Use Stories To Connect Emotionally—it Makes You Relatable   70

20. Be Present—give Your Undivided Attention   72

21. Learn And Remember Personal Details—it Strengthens Rapport   74

22. Show Patience—it Encourages Open Dialogue   77

23. Acknowledge Others' Perspectives—it Shows Respect   79

Contents

24. Build A Sense Of Belonging—it Makes People Feel Valued   81

25. Maintain A Positive Tone—it Makes Interactions Uplifting   83

26. Avoid Interrupting—it Ensures Mutual Respect   85

27. Recognize Achievements Publicly—it Reinforces Connections   87

28. Be Approachable—it Invites Openness   89

29. Keep Promises—it Establishes Credibility   91

30. Share Uplifting Messages Or Resources—it Builds Trust   93

31. Use Humor To Diffuse Tension—it Makes Connections Smoother   95

32. Respect Boundaries—it Ensures Comfort In Relationships   98

33. Use Technology Wisely To Stay In Touch—it Bridges Gaps   101

34. Encourage Others To Share Their Stories—it Builds Trust   104

35. End Conversations On A Positive Note—it Leaves A Lasting Impression   106

"Ways To Influence" Focus On Persuasion, Storytelling, And Negotiation

36. Start With A Powerful Opening Line- It Grabs Attention   111

37. Use "we" Instead Of "I" - To Foster Collaboration   113

38. Share Stories That Resonate Emotionally- Facts Tell, Stories Sell   115

39. Frame Your Ideas With Benefits For The Listener   117

40. Ask Open-ended Questions To Guide The Conversation   119

41. Use The Power Of Pauses- Silence Can Be Persuasive   121

42. Simplify Your Message- Clarity Builds Influence   123

43. Provide Evidence To Back Your Claims- Credibility Matters   125

44. Show Empathy- It Builds Deeper Connections   127

45. Highlight The "why" Behind Your Message- It's What Inspires Action   130

46. Use Metaphors Or Analogies—they Make Complex Ideas Relatable   132

47. Focus On Shared Goals—it Aligns Interests   134

48. Practice Active Listening—it Makes The Other Person Feel Valued   136

49. Present Solutions Rather Than Problems—it Inspires Confidence   138

Contents

50. Anticipate Objections And Address Them Calmly—it Reduces Resistance   140

51. Use Positive Reinforcement—it Encourages Cooperation   143

52. Speak With Conviction—it Enhances Your Authority   146

53. Acknowledge Opposing Views—it Shows Respect And Balance   148

54. Show Enthusiasm—it's Contagious And Motivates Others   150

55. Appeal To Emotions—it Drives Decisions More Than Logic   152

56. Share Relatable Examples—it Creates A Personal Connection   155

57. Create A Sense Of Urgency—it Spurs Action   157

58. Be Adaptable—flexibility Makes Your Influence More Effective   159

59. Use Visuals To Reinforce Your Message—they Boost Retention   162

60. Ask Thought-provoking Questions—it Stimulates Engagement.   164

61. Highlight Long-term Benefits—it Shifts Focus Beyond Immediate Results   167

62. Speak Their Language—adapt To Their Communication Style   170

63. Provide Step-by-step Guidance—it Ensures Clarity And Action   173

64. Use Data Sparingly—it Adds Credibility Without Overwhelming   175

65. Be Consistent In Your Message—it Builds Trust   178

66. Align Your Body Language With Your Words—it Avoids Mixed Signals   180

67. Reinforce Key Points With Repetition—it Solidifies Understanding.   183

68. Build Suspense Before Revealing A Key Idea—it Keeps Attention   187

69. Offer Alternatives—it Empowers Others To Make Decisions   190

70. End With A Strong Call To Action—it Ensures Follow-through   194

"Ways To Inspire" Focus On Motivating Teams, Public Speaking, And Leadership Communication

71. Lead By Example- Your Actions Communicate Louder Than Words   199

72. Use Inspirational Quotes To Uplift Conversations   203

Contents

73. It's Relatable- Share Personal Challenges And How You Overcame Them   207

74. Acknowledge And Celebrate Others' Contributions   211

75. Paint A Vivid Vision Of Success For Your Audience   215

76. Speak With Passion- It's Contagious   219

77. Use Humor- It Breaks Barriers And Creates A Positive Atmosphere   223

78. Give Constructive Feedback With A Positive Tone   227

79. Adapt Your Communication Style To Suit The Audience   231

80. Cultivate A Culture Of Growth- It Drives Results   236

81. Share Success Stories From Others—it Motivates And Builds Belief   238

82. Encourage Collaboration—it Fosters Collective Achievement   240

83. Recognize Potential In People Before They See It Themselves   243

84. Inspire With Questions That Spark Creative Thinking   245

85. Speak To The Heart Before Appealing To The Mind—it Connects Deeply   247

86. Use Storytelling To Convey Lessons And Inspire Change   249

87. Remind Others Of Their Progress—it Fuels Perseverance   251

88. Empower Others To Take Ownership—it Builds Confidence   253

89. Address Fears And Offer Reassurance—it Strengthens Resolve   255

90. Set High Expectations—it Challenges People To Rise Above   258

91. Acknowledge Effort, Not Just Results—it Encourages Persistence   260

92. Show Vulnerability—it Makes You Relatable And Authentic   262

93. Use Metaphors To Simplify Complex Ideas—it Creates Clarity   264

94. Encourage People To Dream Big—it Expands Possibilities   266

95. Share Your "why"—it Adds Meaning To The Journey   268

96. Highlight The Impact Of Their Work—it Boosts Morale   270

97. Be Genuine And Sincere—it Builds Trust And Loyalty   272

98. Create A Safe Space For Sharing Ideas—it Fosters Innovation   275

Contents

99. Inspire Through Action—demonstrate The Behaviors You Want To See 277

100. Offer Hope During Tough Times—it Instills Resilience 279

101. Remind Others Of Their Unique Strengths—it Inspires Self-belief 281

Connecting, influencing, and inspiring are lifelong journeys 285

Foreword

In today's fast-paced world, the ability to communicate effectively is more important than ever. Whether you're leading a team, giving a presentation, or simply having a conversation, how you express yourself shapes your relationships and influences the way others perceive you.

This book, "Speak with Impact," is not just a guide to communication—it's a practical roadmap to becoming a more confident and powerful communicator.

Inside, you'll find 101 strategies that can be used every day, no matter where you are in your journey. These techniques are straightforward, easy to understand, and most importantly, they work. They have the power to help you connect with others on a deeper level, inspire action, and leave a lasting impression.

But more than just strategies, this book invites you to step into your full potential as a communicator. It's about developing the skills to lead with authenticity, to speak with clarity, and to inspire those around you to take action.

I hope that as you read through these pages, you'll find ways to improve your communication, connect more deeply with others, and begin to make a greater impact in all areas of your life.

Take these strategies, apply them, and watch the change unfold. Your journey to speaking with impact starts now.

Preface

We all have a voice, but how often do we truly use it to connect, influence, and inspire? So many of us struggle with expressing ourselves clearly, or fear that our words won't have the impact we hope for. But the truth is, everyone has the ability to speak with power and purpose. It's a skill that can be developed and refined.

This book is my gift to you—a collection of 101 practical strategies designed to help you communicate with confidence, connect deeply with others, and inspire action in ways you may not have thought possible.

Each strategy is simple, actionable, and backed by real-world examples. Whether you're a business leader, a student, or someone who just wants to improve how they express themselves, these strategies are meant to be tools you can use right away.

However this book is more than just about tips and techniques. It's about encouraging you to find your voice, to speak with authenticity, and to realize that your words can create meaningful change in both your personal and professional life.

I want you to read this not just to gain knowledge, but to start using what you learn to make an impact right now. The strategies here are meant to be tried, tested, and lived.

So, let's get started. Let's speak with impact and make the difference we were always meant to make.

Acknowledgements

Writing this book has been an incredible journey, and I couldn't have done it without the support and encouragement of many wonderful people.

First, I want to thank my church, family and friends for always believing in me. Your unwavering support and love have kept me going even when the path seemed difficult. To my colleagues at M Square Motivation, thank you for inspiring me every day to keep pushing boundaries and helping others grow.

I'd also like to acknowledge the countless mentors, coaches, and individuals who have shared their wisdom with me over the years. Your guidance has shaped the way I think about communication and leadership.

To my readers—thank you for trusting me with your time and attention. This book is for you. I hope it serves you as a tool to create lasting change in your life, and I hope it helps you find the confidence to speak with impact in every situation.

Finally, a special thanks to everyone who has been a part of my journey, from the smallest gesture to the most significant influence. Your presence has made this possible.

Prologue

The Power of the Spoken Word!

They are the building blocks of our reality, the currency of connection, and the weapons of influence. In the symphony of human interaction, the spoken word reigns supreme. It can mend broken hearts, ignite revolutions, and sway the course of history.

Imagine a world without the power of speech. A world devoid of stories, debates, and the simple joy of sharing ideas. It would be a sterile, lifeless place, a pale shadow of the vibrant tapestry we inhabit.

This book is your guide to unlocking the full potential of your voice. Within these pages, you'll discover 101 strategies to connect with your audience, wield the art of persuasion, and ignite a spark of inspiration within others.

Whether you're a seasoned orator or someone who simply wants to improve their communication skills, "Speak with Impact" will equip you with the tools and techniques to become a more confident, compelling, and influential speaker.

Get ready to unleash the power of your voice and leave an indelible mark on the world.

"Ways to Connect" Focus on building relationships, trust, and rapport

ONE

SMILE- IT'S YOUR FIRST CONNECTION TOOL

Have you ever noticed how a simple smile can brighten someone's day? It's like magic, really. It's like you're waving a little wand and instantly making someone feel a bit better.

Think about it. You're walking down the street, maybe feeling a little down, and then someone smiles at you. Suddenly, you feel a little lighter, a little happier. It's amazing how something so small can have such a big impact.

That's the power of a smile. It's a universal language. Everyone understands it. Babies smile back at you, even when they don't know you. It's like we're all wired to connect through smiles.

And it's not just about making others feel good. Smiling actually makes you feel good too! It tricks your brain into releasing happy chemicals, so you end up feeling happier yourself.

So, next time you're feeling down, try forcing a smile. It might feel silly at first, but trust me, it works. And don't forget to smile at the people you meet throughout your day. It might make their day a little brighter, and it will definitely make yours.

Remember: A smile is a superpower. Use it wisely.

ᕤᕤᕤ

The Science of Smiles

Okay, let's get a little bit more scientific here. Did you know that smiling actually triggers a chain reaction in your brain? It's true!

When you smile, your brain releases these amazing chemicals called endorphins. Think of them as your body's natural happy pills. These endorphins make you feel good, relaxed, and even a little bit euphoric.

But that's not all! Smiling also helps to lower your stress levels. When you're stressed, your body releases a hormone called cortisol. Cortisol can make you feel anxious, irritable, and even physically unwell. But when you smile, it helps to counteract the effects of cortisol, calming your body and mind.

So, not only does smiling make you feel good, but it also helps you stay healthy! Pretty amazing, right?

ᗷᗷᗷ

Smiling Your Way to Connection

Now, let's talk about the social magic of smiles.

Have you ever noticed how smiling makes you seem more approachable? It's like you're putting up a little sign that says, "Come talk to me! I'm friendly!"

When you smile at someone, you're sending a clear message that you're open and welcoming. It makes them feel more comfortable around you and more likely to want to engage in conversation.

Think about it. Would you rather talk to someone who is frowning or someone who is smiling? Most people would choose the person who is smiling, right?

Smiling also helps to build trust and rapport. When you smile at someone, it shows that you're genuine and sincere. It makes them feel valued and appreciated.

ᗷᗷᗷ

Mastering the Art of the Smile

Okay, now it's time to put your newfound knowledge to the test! How do you actually master the art of smiling?

Practice Makes Perfect:

Look in the mirror and practice your smile. Does it look genuine? Or does it look a bit forced?

Experiment with different types of smiles. A gentle smile, a warm smile, a playful smile.

Smile at Strangers:

Make a conscious effort to smile at people you encounter throughout your day. The cashier at the grocery store, the barista at the coffee shop, the dog walker you pass on the street.

You might be surprised at how many smiles you get in return.

Bring Your Smile to Conversations:

When you're talking to someone, remember to smile. It shows that you're engaged and interested in what they have to say.

Make eye contact and smile while you're listening. It makes the other person feel heard and valued.

ᗏᗏᗏ

The Unexpected Benefits of Smiling

You might be surprised to learn that smiling has some unexpected benefits.

Reduced Pain: Studies have shown that smiling can actually help to reduce pain.

Boosted Immunity: Believe it or not, smiling can actually boost your immune system!

Increased Creativity: When you're feeling happy and relaxed (thanks to those endorphins!), your creativity tends to flow more freely.

So, not only does smiling make you more likable and happier, but it can also improve your physical and mental health!

ᗏᗏᗏ

Spreading the Smile

I believe that the world would be a much better place if everyone smiled a little more. So, let's make it a mission to spread the smile!

Smile at yourself in the mirror every morning.

Make an effort to smile at at least one new person every day.

Encourage others to smile more.

Let's work together to create a world where smiles are contagious!

ᗏᗏᗏ

The Many Faces of Smiles

Did you know there are actually different types of smiles? It's true! Each smile conveys a unique message and evokes different emotions. Here are a few examples:

<u>The Genuine Smile (Duchenne Smile)</u>: This is the real deal! It involves not only the muscles around your mouth but also the muscles around your eyes. This creates those lovely crinkles around the eyes, which are a sure sign of genuine happiness.

<u>The Social Smile</u>: This is the polite smile we use in social situations. It's a friendly and appropriate smile, but it may not always reflect true inner feelings.

<u>The Grimace Smile</u>: This is a forced smile, often used when we feel uncomfortable or awkward. It's a bit of a tense smile, and it doesn't exactly radiate joy.

<u>The Sad Smile</u>: This is a subtle smile that can accompany sadness or melancholy. It's a bittersweet smile, often used to mask deeper emotions.

Pay attention to the different types of smiles you encounter throughout your day. Notice how they make you feel.

ᗰᗰᗰ

Overcoming Shyness and Smiling Confidently

For some people, smiling can feel a bit awkward, especially if they're shy or introverted. But don't worry! There are ways to overcome this shyness and smile more confidently.

<u>Start Small</u>: Begin by smiling at yourself in the mirror. It might feel a bit silly at first, but it can help you become more comfortable with the feeling of smiling.

<u>Focus on Others</u>: Instead of focusing on yourself, try to focus on the other person. What are they saying? How are they feeling? This can help to take the pressure off and allow your smile to come more naturally.

<u>Practice Mindfulness</u>: Pay attention to the feeling of smiling. Notice how it makes you feel. Try to connect with the positive emotions that arise when you smile.

Remember, confidence comes with practice. The more you smile, the more natural it will feel.

ᗰᗰᗰ

The Power of a Genuine Smile

A genuine smile has the power to transform lives. It can:

<u>Build stronger relationships</u>: Genuine smiles foster deeper connections with others. They build trust, create a sense of warmth, and make people feel valued and appreciated.

<u>Create a positive atmosphere</u>: When you smile, you create a positive atmosphere around you. It's contagious! Your smile can uplift the mood of those around you and create a more enjoyable and pleasant experience for everyone.

<u>Make the world a brighter place</u>: Imagine a world filled with genuine smiles. Wouldn't that be a wonderful place to live? Every smile, no matter how small, contributes to a more positive and joyful world.

So, let's make a conscious effort to spread more genuine smiles. Let's use our smiles to connect, to inspire, and to make the world a brighter place for everyone.

ᗡᗡᗡ

TWO

Use the person's name in conversations- It shows you value them

Have you ever noticed how it feels when someone uses your name in conversation? It's a subtle thing, but it can have a surprisingly powerful effect. Suddenly, you feel more engaged, more valued, and more connected to the person you're talking to.

Think about it. When you're in a conversation, and the other person uses your name, it's like they're saying, "I'm paying attention to you. I'm interested in what you have to say. And I value your opinion."

It's a simple gesture, but it can make a world of difference.

ᚦᚦᚦ

The Magic of Personalization

Using someone's name is like adding a personal touch to the conversation. It's like saying, "I see you. I recognize you as an individual."

Imagine you're at a party, and you're talking to a group of people. One person keeps using your name, while the others seem to be talking at you rather than to you. Who are you more likely to remember? Who are you more likely to connect with?

The answer is simple: the person who used your name.

ๆๆๆ

The Science of Connection

Using someone's name isn't just about politeness; it has a real impact on our brains. When we hear our own name, it triggers a sense of recognition and importance. It makes us feel seen, heard, and valued.

This can have a significant impact on our interactions. When we feel valued, we're more likely to open up, share our thoughts and feelings, and build deeper connections with others.

ๆๆๆ

Mastering the Art of Using Names

Now, let's learn how to master the art of using names effectively:

Use it Naturally: Don't force it. Use someone's name naturally throughout the conversation, as appropriate.

Avoid Overuse: Overusing someone's name can feel unnatural and even a bit creepy.

Combine with Other Techniques: Combine using someone's name with other active listening techniques, such as making eye contact, nodding, and summarizing their points.

For example, instead of saying, "That's a great point," you could say, "That's a great point, David."

ๆๆๆ

The Ripple Effect

Using someone's name can have a ripple effect. When you use someone's name, it not only makes them feel valued, but it also creates a more positive and engaging atmosphere for everyone involved.

So, the next time you're in a conversation, remember the power of a name. Use it wisely, and watch your connections deepen.

ๆๆๆ

Names Across Cultures

The way we use names varies significantly across different cultures. In some cultures, it's considered very formal to use someone's first name, while in others, it's seen as a sign of friendliness and informality.

<u>Formal vs. Informal</u>: In some cultures, using someone's first name too soon can be seen as disrespectful. It's important to observe social cues and wait for the appropriate time to transition from formal (Mr./Ms./Dr. + Last Name) to first name.

<u>Titles and Honorifics</u>: Many cultures place a strong emphasis on titles and honorifics. For example, in many Asian cultures, using someone's family name as a sign of respect.

<u>Addressing Elders</u>: In many cultures, there are specific rules for addressing elders. This might involve using honorifics, titles, or even avoiding using their first name altogether.

It's crucial to be mindful of cultural differences and adapt your approach accordingly. When in doubt, it's always best to err on the side of formality.

ppp

The Impact of Names on Memory and Recall

Using someone's name not only strengthens your connection with them but also improves your ability to remember them.

<u>The Names Game</u>: When you use someone's name, it creates a stronger association between their name and their face. This makes it easier to recall their name later on.

<u>Enhanced Memory</u>: Using someone's name during a conversation helps to anchor the conversation in your memory. You're more likely to remember the key points of the conversation if you can associate them with the person's name.

<u>Improved Attention</u>: When you use someone's name, it forces you to pay closer attention to them and the conversation. This increased focus can lead to better memory and recall.

By consciously using someone's name, you can enhance your memory and recall, making your interactions more meaningful and memorable.

ppp

Remembering Names with Ease

Remembering names can be challenging, but with a few simple techniques, you can significantly improve your recall:

<u>Repeat the Name</u>: When you first meet someone, repeat their name back to them. For example, "Nice to meet you, David." This helps to solidify the name in your mind.

<u>Associate the Name with a Unique Feature</u>: Try to associate the person's name with a unique feature about them. For example, if you meet someone named "John Smith" who is wearing a bright red tie, you can associate the name "John" with the color "red."

<u>Use Mnemonic Devices</u>: Create a simple mnemonic device to help you remember the name. For example, if you meet someone named "David," you could associate their name with the word "dove," which starts with the same sound.

<u>Practice Active Listening</u>: Pay close attention to the person and the conversation. When you're truly engaged, remembering their name becomes easier.

By incorporating these techniques into your interactions, you can become more confident in remembering names and build stronger, more meaningful connections with others.

ppp

THREE

ACTIVE LISTENING-LISTEN TO UNDERSTAND, NOT JUST REPLY

We often think of communication as a one-way street – we talk, and others listen. But true communication is a two-way street. It requires active listening, which means listening to understand, not just to reply.

Active listening is more than just hearing the words someone is saying. It's about paying close attention to their message, both verbal and non-verbal, and demonstrating that you're truly engaged.

ꝓꝓꝓ

The Power of Presence:

When you actively listen, you're fully present in the moment. You're not distracted by your phone, your thoughts, or your to-do list. You're focused on the other person and what they have to say.

This presence creates a safe and supportive space for the other person to open up and share their thoughts and feelings. It shows them that you value their perspective and that you're genuinely interested in what they have to say.

Key Elements of Active Listening:

<u>Pay Attention</u>: Give the speaker your full attention. Make eye contact, nod your head, and avoid distractions.

<u>Listen with Empathy</u>: Try to understand the speaker's perspective, even if you don't agree with them. Put yourself in their shoes and try to see things from their point of view.

<u>Ask Clarifying Questions</u>: If you're unsure about something, don't hesitate to ask clarifying questions. This shows that you're truly engaged and that you want to understand their message fully.

<u>Summarize and Reflect</u>: Summarize the speaker's main points to ensure that you've understood them correctly. Reflect their feelings back to them. For example, "It sounds like you're feeling frustrated because..."

Avoid Interrupting: Let the speaker finish their thoughts before you respond. Avoid interrupting them or trying to steer the conversation in a different direction.

The Benefits of Active Listening

Active listening has numerous benefits:

<u>Stronger Relationships</u>: Active listening builds stronger, more meaningful relationships. It fosters trust, intimacy, and understanding.

<u>Improved Communication</u>: Active listening helps to avoid misunderstandings and improve the overall quality of communication.

<u>Increased Empathy and Compassion</u>: By truly listening to others, we develop greater empathy and compassion for their experiences.

<u>Reduced Conflict</u>: Active listening can help to de-escalate conflicts and resolve disagreements more effectively.

Active listening is a valuable skill that can enhance all aspects of our lives. By practicing active listening, we can improve our relationships, strengthen our communication skills, and build a more connected and compassionate world.

ନ୍ନନ୍ନନ୍ନ

Overcoming Common Listening Barriers

We all face distractions that can hinder our ability to actively listen. Here are some common listening barriers and how to overcome them:

Distractions:

<u>External Distractions</u>: Minimize external distractions as much as possible. Find a quiet space to talk, turn off your phone, and avoid interruptions.

<u>Internal Distractions</u>: Minimize internal distractions such as racing thoughts or worries. Practice mindfulness techniques to quiet your mind and focus on the present moment.

Prejudices and Assumptions:

Be aware of your own biases and assumptions. Try to listen to the speaker with an open mind and avoid jumping to conclusions.

Challenge your assumptions and be willing to consider different perspectives.

Emotional Reactions:

If you're feeling strong emotions (anger, sadness, etc.), take a moment to calm down before engaging in the conversation.

Acknowledge your emotions, but don't let them cloud your judgment or prevent you from truly listening.

Thinking About Your Response:

Resist the urge to formulate your response while the other person is still speaking. Focus on understanding their message first.

Take notes if necessary, but don't let note-taking distract you from the conversation.

By identifying and overcoming these common listening barriers, you can significantly improve your ability to actively listen and connect with others.

ϷϷϷ

The Role of Body Language in Active Listening

Body language plays a crucial role in active listening. It communicates our level of engagement and interest. Here are some key body language cues that demonstrate active listening:

Maintain Eye Contact: Make and maintain eye contact with the speaker, but avoid staring intensely.

Nod Your Head: Nod your head occasionally to show that you're following and understanding.

Use Open Body Language: Keep your arms and legs uncrossed. Lean slightly forward to show that you're engaged.

Mirror the Speaker's Body Language: (Subtly) mirroring the speaker's body language can help to build rapport and create a sense of connection.

Conversely, avoid closed-off body language such as crossing your arms, avoiding eye contact, or looking around the room. These cues can signal disinterest and make the speaker feel unheard.

ϷϷϷ

Active Listening in Everyday Life

Active listening is a valuable skill in all aspects of life:

<u>Relationships</u>: Active listening strengthens personal and professional relationships. It fosters intimacy, trust, and understanding in romantic relationships, friendships, and family dynamics.

<u>Work</u>: Active listening is essential for effective communication in the workplace. It improves teamwork, enhances problem-solving, and builds stronger relationships with colleagues and clients.

<u>Parenting</u>: Active listening is crucial for effective parenting. It helps parents to understand their children's needs and feelings, build strong bonds, and guide them through life's challenges.

By incorporating active listening into your daily interactions, you can improve your communication skills, build stronger relationships, and create a more positive and fulfilling life.

ϷϷϷ

FOUR

MAINTAIN EYE CONTACT- IT CREATES TRUST

Imagine this: you're telling a friend about the most amazing concert you went to. You're getting excited, describing the music, the energy of the crowd, everything! But as you talk, you notice your friend looking away, distracted. Maybe they're checking their phone or looking around the room. How does that make you feel? A little deflated, maybe? Like your story isn't interesting or that they're not really paying attention.

Now, picture this: you're sharing your story, and your friend is looking you directly in the eyes, nodding along, and even leaning forward, clearly captivated by what you're saying. You feel valued, heard, and connected. That's the magic of eye contact.

ᘒᘒᘒ

More Than Just Looking:
Eye contact is more than just looking at someone; it's a powerful way to connect on a deeper level. It's like a silent language that communicates interest, honesty, and empathy.

<u>The Magic of Connection</u>: When we make eye contact, our brains release special chemicals that help us feel connected to the other person. It's like a subtle dance, where our gazes meet and create a sense of intimacy and understanding.

<u>Building Trust</u>: Genuine eye contact builds trust. When someone looks you directly in the eyes, it shows they're honest and sincere. It makes you feel like they're truly present in the moment and invested in the conversation.

<u>A Window to the Soul</u>: Our eyes can reveal a lot about our emotions. When you look closely at someone's eyes, you can often see if they're happy, sad, or even a little nervous. This helps you understand them better and build stronger connections.

ԲԲԲ

Mastering the Art of the Look

<u>Find Your Comfort Zone</u>: Don't stare intensely! It can feel a bit awkward. Instead, find a comfortable rhythm where you're making and holding eye contact, but also allowing your gaze to naturally shift around their face.

<u>Beyond the Eyes</u>: While maintaining eye contact, gently shift your gaze to their forehead, nose, and mouth. This creates a more natural and engaging interaction.

<u>Cultural Considerations</u>: It's important to remember that eye contact norms vary across cultures. In some cultures, prolonged eye contact is considered respectful, while in others, it may be seen as a bit aggressive.

ԲԲԲ

The benefits of good eye contact go beyond just making someone feel heard.

<u>Stronger Relationships</u>: Eye contact strengthens bonds with friends, family, and loved ones. It creates a sense of intimacy and trust that deepens your connections.

<u>Improved Communication</u>: When you make eye contact, you're more likely to understand and be understood. It helps you truly listen and respond thoughtfully.

<u>Increased Confidence</u>: Maintaining confident eye contact can boost your own self-esteem. It shows that you value yourself and your opinions.

Eye contact is a simple yet powerful tool that can significantly enhance our communication and relationships. By mastering the art of the look, we can create deeper connections, build trust, and make our interactions more meaningful and enjoyable. So, the next time you're in conversation, remember the power of a genuine gaze. It can make all the difference.

ԲԲԲ

We've explored how eye contact builds trust and fosters connection, but its impact goes far beyond simple communication.

The Power of Presence: Maintaining eye contact signals that you are truly present in the moment. You're not distracted by your phone, your thoughts, or the world around you. You're fully engaged with the person you're speaking with, showing them that they have your undivided attention.

A Confidence Booster: Making eye contact can actually boost your own confidence. When you look someone in the eyes, you project an image of assertiveness and self-assurance. This can be especially helpful in situations where you need to assert yourself, such as during a presentation or a negotiation.

Eye Contact and Empathy: Eye contact allows us to connect with the emotions of others on a deeper level. By observing the subtle shifts in someone's gaze, we can gain valuable insights into their feelings. Are they looking away because they're feeling shy? Are they avoiding eye contact because they're feeling uncomfortable or stressed? Paying attention to these cues can help us to understand and empathize with others more deeply.

ᑭᑭᑭ

Beyond the Basics: The Art of the Subtle Gaze

The Power of the Pause: A brief pause in eye contact can add a layer of depth to the conversation. It can create a moment of reflection or allow the other person to process their thoughts.

The Art of the Glance: Gentle glances away from the eyes, such as to the forehead or nose, can create a more natural and less intense interaction.

Cultural Nuances: It's crucial to remember that eye contact norms vary significantly across cultures. In some cultures, prolonged eye contact is considered disrespectful, while in others, it's a sign of respect and engagement.

ᑭᑭᑭ

Eye Contact in a Digital World:

In the age of video calls and online meetings, maintaining eye contact can be a bit more challenging. However, it's still crucial.

Look at the Camera: When on a video call, try to look directly into the camera lens. This gives the impression that you are making eye contact with the other person.

<u>Minimize Distractions</u>: Minimize distractions during video calls to ensure that you can maintain focus and make meaningful eye contact.

Eye contact is a powerful and multifaceted tool that goes beyond simple communication. It's a window to the soul, a bridge to connection, and a key to building stronger, more meaningful relationships. By mastering the art of eye contact, we can enhance our communication skills, build trust, and create a more positive and engaging experience for ourselves and others.

ᗰᗰᗰ

FIVE

MIRROR THEIR BODY LANGUAGE- IT BUILDS RAPPORT

Have you ever noticed how sometimes, when you're talking to someone, you seem to fall into a natural rhythm? You might unconsciously lean forward when they lean forward, or cross your legs when they cross theirs. This isn't just a coincidence; it's a fascinating phenomenon called mirroring.

Think of it like this: when you're playing music with a band, you naturally adjust your tempo and rhythm to match the other musicians. Mirroring is like that, but with your body language. It's a subtle way of saying, "I'm with you. I understand you. I'm on the same wavelength."

ᗝᗝᗝ

Why Does Mirroring Work?

<u>Building Bridges of Understanding</u>: When you subtly mirror someone's body language – leaning forward when they lean forward, mirroring their pace of speech – you create a sense of harmony and connection. It's like you're speaking the same unspoken language.

<u>Boosting Empathy</u>: Mirroring helps you understand the other person on a deeper level. When you mirror their posture and gestures, you're more likely to feel what they're feeling. It's like you're stepping into their shoes for a moment.

<u>Creating a Sense of Liking</u>: We naturally gravitate towards people who seem similar to us. When you subtly mirror someone's body language, you

create a sense of similarity, making them feel more comfortable and connected to you.

❦❦❦

The Art of Subtle Mirroring

<u>Be a Chameleon, Not a Copycat</u>: Mirroring should be subtle and natural. Don't become a caricature of the other person!

<u>Focus on Subtle Cues</u>: Pay attention to small things like leaning forward, crossing legs, nodding, or adjusting their posture.

<u>Match Their Energy</u>: If they're speaking slowly and calmly, mirror their relaxed pace. If they're more energetic and animated, let your energy level rise a bit.

<u>Read the Room</u>: Pay attention to how the other person reacts. If they seem uncomfortable with your mirroring, back off a bit.

❦❦❦

Mirroring Beyond Body Language

Mirroring isn't just about physical gestures. You can also subtly mirror someone's speech patterns, tone of voice, and even their vocabulary. For example, if they use a certain phrase or word repeatedly, you can subtly incorporate it into your own conversation.

The Bottom Line

Mirroring is a powerful, subconscious tool that can enhance your communication and build stronger relationships. It's about creating a sense of connection and understanding, not about mimicking someone else. So, the next time you're in conversation, pay attention to your body language and the body language of the other person. You might be surprised at how subtle mirroring can deepen your connections and enhance your interactions.

❦❦❦

The Unconscious Connection

Mirroring is a subconscious way of saying, "I'm with you. I understand you. I'm on the same wavelength." When we subtly mirror someone's body language – their posture, their gestures, even their tone of voice – we're creating a sense of harmony and connection. It's like speaking a secret language of nonverbal communication.

<u>Building Rapport on a Deeper Level</u>: Mirroring goes beyond just polite conversation. It creates a sense of rapport that goes deeper than words. It fosters a feeling of trust, comfort, and understanding.

<u>The Empathy Boost</u>: When you mirror someone's body language, you're not just observing their actions; you're almost feeling them. This subtle mimicry activates our mirror neurons, which allow us to understand and even feel the emotions of others.

<u>Creating a Sense of Liking and Trust</u>: We are naturally drawn to people who seem similar to us. When you subtly mirror someone's body language, you create a sense of shared experience and similarity, making them feel more comfortable and connected to you.

ϷϷϷ

The Ethical Considerations of Mirroring

While mirroring can be a powerful tool for building rapport and enhancing communication, it's important to use it ethically and mindfully.

<u>The Line Between Connection and Manipulation</u>: Subtle mirroring is a natural and unconscious way to connect with others. However, overt or deliberate mirroring can come across as manipulative or insincere.

<u>Respecting Individuality</u>: Everyone communicates differently. While subtle mirroring can enhance connection, it's crucial to respect individual boundaries and communication styles. Avoid mimicking someone to the point where they feel uncomfortable or manipulated.

<u>Cultural Sensitivity</u>: Mirroring norms vary across cultures. In some cultures, mirroring may be considered a sign of respect and engagement, while in others, it may be seen as intrusive or even disrespectful.

ϷϷϷ

When Mirroring Might Not Be Appropriate:

<u>Interviews and Negotiations</u>: In high-stakes situations like job interviews or negotiations, overt mirroring can be perceived as manipulative or even manipulative.

<u>Intimidating Situations</u>: If the other person seems uncomfortable or intimidated, it's best to avoid mirroring.

<u>With People Who Have Social Anxiety</u>: Overly mirroring someone with social anxiety can make them feel uncomfortable or self-conscious.

ϷϷϷ

Mirroring with Authenticity

The key to ethical mirroring lies in authenticity. Focus on genuine connection and understanding, rather than trying to manipulate or control the interaction. Allow your mirroring to flow naturally from your genuine interest in the other person and the conversation.

Mirroring is a powerful tool for building rapport and enhancing communication. However, it's crucial to use it ethically and mindfully. By being aware of the potential pitfalls and respecting individual boundaries, you can harness the power of mirroring to create deeper, more meaningful connections with the people around you.

PPP

Mirroring in the Digital Age: Navigating the New Landscape

Technology has profoundly impacted the way we communicate, and mirroring is no exception. While face-to-face interactions still reign supreme for nuanced mirroring, the digital age presents both challenges and new opportunities.

The Challenges of Mirroring in the Digital Age:

Limited Nonverbal Cues: In text-based communication, we lose many of the subtle nonverbal cues that facilitate mirroring. Tone of voice, body language, and even facial expressions are often lost in translation.

The Illusion of Presence: While video calls offer a glimpse into nonverbal communication, they can still be limited. Distractions like poor internet connection and background noise can hinder our ability to accurately perceive and mirror subtle cues.

The Rise of Emojis and GIFs: Emojis and GIFs can be used to convey emotions and mimic certain facial expressions, but they can also be overused or misinterpreted, leading to misunderstandings.

PPP

Opportunities for Mirroring in the Digital Age:

Mirroring Tone and Pace: Even in text-based communication, we can subtly mirror the other person's tone and pace. If they are using short, concise sentences, we can adjust our own writing style accordingly.

Using Emojis and GIFs Sparingly: When used thoughtfully, emojis and GIFs can help to convey tone and emotion, enhancing the mirroring experience.

<u>Focusing on Active Listening</u>: In video calls, pay close attention to the other person's facial expressions, tone of voice, and body language. Try to mirror their energy level and adjust your own communication style accordingly.

The Importance of Authenticity in the Digital Age:

In the digital age, it's crucial to maintain authenticity in our communication. Avoid overly trying to mirror someone online, especially if it feels forced or inauthentic. Focus on genuine connection and meaningful communication, rather than trying to manipulate the interaction.

Technology has presented new challenges and opportunities for mirroring. While the nuances of nonverbal communication may be more difficult to capture in the digital world, we can still adapt and find ways to connect authentically with others. By paying attention to subtle cues, using digital tools thoughtfully, and focusing on genuine connection, we can continue to harness the power of mirroring in the digital age.

ϷϷϷ

SIX

FIND COMMON GROUND IN CONVERSATIONS-START WITH SHARED INTERESTS

Have you ever felt like you're talking to a brick wall? You're sharing a fascinating anecdote about your weekend hiking adventure, brimming with excitement, while the other person offers polite nods and quickly steers the conversation elsewhere. It's a familiar feeling – that of disconnection, of your enthusiasm falling flat.

But what if I told you there's a secret ingredient to truly engaging conversations? It's not about being the most eloquent speaker or having the most fascinating life story. It's about finding common ground, those shared threads that weave a tapestry of connection between you and the other person.

Imagine this: you're at a social gathering, and you overhear someone passionately discussing their latest culinary creation – homemade pasta from scratch! Now, if you're a fellow foodie, your ears perk up. You might find yourself exclaiming, "Oh, I'm a huge pasta enthusiast myself! I've been meaning to try making ravioli. What kind of pasta did you make?" Suddenly, a spark ignites. You've found common ground, and the conversation flows effortlessly, filled with shared excitement and genuine interest.

ᐅᐅᐅ

The Art of Discovering Shared Terrain

Finding common ground is like unearthing hidden treasures. It requires a curious mind, a keen ear, and a willingness to delve beneath the surface.

Become a Master Listener: Pay close attention to what the other person is saying. What are their passions? What are they excited about? What kind of music do they listen to? What books are they reading? These seemingly small details can offer valuable clues about their interests and values.

Ask Questions That Go Beyond the Surface: Instead of asking closed-ended questions like, "Do you like to travel?" delve deeper with questions like, "What's the most memorable trip you've ever taken?" or "What do you love most about exploring new places?"

Share Your Own Story Authentically: Don't be afraid to share your own passions and interests. This not only makes you more relatable but also invites the other person to connect with you on a deeper level. Perhaps you both share a love for independent films, a fascination with ancient history, or a passion for rescuing shelter animals.

Look for the Unexpected Connections: Sometimes, the most interesting connections are the ones you least expect. You might discover a shared love for obscure documentaries, a mutual appreciation for the same quirky sense of humor, or a surprising connection through a shared life experience.

ᐅᐅᐅ

The Power of Shared Experiences

Shared experiences create a powerful bond. They provide a common ground for understanding, empathy, and shared memories.

Travel Tales: Have you both visited the same city? Share your favorite local spots, compare your travel experiences, and reminisce about the unique sights and sounds that captivated you.

Life's Milestones: Have you both gone through similar life experiences, such as raising children, changing careers, or overcoming a challenging personal hurdle? Sharing these experiences can create a deep sense of understanding and connection, fostering empathy and a sense of shared humanity.

Shared Interests: Whether it's a love for cooking, a passion for sports, a shared interest in a particular hobby, or a fascination with a specific historical period, shared interests provide fertile ground for engaging and meaningful conversations.

ᗡᗡᗡ

Finding Common Ground: A Two-Way Street

Remember, finding common ground is a collaborative effort. It requires active listening, genuine curiosity, and a willingness to share your own authentic self. By cultivating this skill, you can transform any conversation into a more meaningful and enjoyable experience. You'll not only connect with others on a deeper level but also enrich your own life by discovering new interests and perspectives.

The Art of Asking Insightful Questions: Unlocking Deeper Connections

Imagine a conversation where you merely exchange pleasantries and offer generic responses. It's likely to feel a bit flat, like two ships passing in the night. Now, picture a conversation where you delve deeper, asking insightful questions that encourage the other person to open up and share their thoughts and feelings. This is where the magic happens.

Asking insightful questions is like wielding a key that unlocks deeper levels of connection. It transforms a simple exchange of words into a meaningful dialogue, where both parties feel heard, understood, and valued.

The Power of the Inquisitive Mind:

<u>Beyond the Surface Level</u>: Insightful questions go beyond the superficial. Instead of asking "How was your weekend?", try asking "What was the highlight of your weekend?" or "What did you do that brought you the most joy?"

<u>Encouraging Deeper Exploration</u>: These questions encourage the other person to delve deeper, to share their thoughts, feelings, and experiences with greater depth and nuance.

<u>Building Rapport</u>: By asking insightful questions, you demonstrate genuine interest in the other person. You're showing that you value their thoughts, opinions, and experiences. This fosters a sense of connection and builds rapport.

<u>Uncovering Hidden Gems</u>: Often, the most interesting conversations arise from unexpected turns. By asking insightful questions, you can uncover hidden passions, surprising stories, and unexpected common ground.

Mastering the Art of the Question:

Open-Ended Questions are Key: Avoid yes-or-no questions. Instead, ask open-ended questions that begin with "What," "How," "Why," "Tell me more about..." or "What are your thoughts on..."

Active Listening is Crucial: Pay close attention to their responses. Listen not just to the words, but also to their tone of voice, their body language, and the emotions they convey.

Build on Their Responses: Use their answers as a springboard for further exploration. Ask follow-up questions that show you're genuinely interested and engaged in the conversation.

Be a Curious Explorer: Approach each conversation with a sense of curiosity and a desire to learn. Ask questions that challenge your own assumptions and broaden your understanding of the world.

Asking insightful questions is not just about gathering information; it's about creating a meaningful and enriching experience for both parties. It fosters deeper connections, builds stronger relationships, and cultivates a sense of understanding and empathy.

By mastering the art of asking insightful questions, you can transform any conversation from a mundane exchange into a vibrant and rewarding experience. So, the next time you find yourself in conversation, remember the power of a well-crafted question. It can unlock a world of insights and deepen your connections in ways you never imagined.

ϷϷϷ

Active Listening: The Cornerstone of Meaningful Conversations

Imagine this: you're excitedly recounting a funny anecdote, eager to share the laughter with a friend. But instead of soaking in your story, they're already formulating their own response, their eyes glazing over as they wait for their turn to speak.

This scenario highlights a common communication pitfall: the failure to truly listen. Active listening is more than just hearing the words someone is saying. It's about truly engaging with their message, understanding their perspective, and showing them that you value their thoughts and feelings.

Beyond Hearing: The Art of True Listening

Active listening is like a superpower. It allows you to connect with others on a deeper level, build stronger relationships, and resolve conflicts more effectively.

More Than Just Words: Active listening involves paying attention to the entire message, not just the words being spoken. Notice their tone of voice, their body language, and the emotions they're conveying.

Putting Yourself in Their Shoes: Try to understand the speaker's perspective, even if you don't agree with them. Imagine yourself in their situation and try to see things from their point of view.

Show You're Engaged: Let the speaker know that you're truly listening. Nod your head, make eye contact, and use verbal cues like "I see," "That's interesting," and "Tell me more."

Reflect and Summarize: To ensure you've understood correctly, summarize the speaker's main points in your own words. This shows that you've been paying attention and that you value their perspective.

 PPP

Overcoming Listening Barriers

The Distractions: Put away your phone, turn off the TV, and find a quiet space where you can give the speaker your undivided attention.

The Inner Critic: Quiet the inner voice that's constantly planning your response or formulating counterarguments.

Emotional Reactions: If you're feeling strong emotions (anger, frustration, etc.), take a moment to calm down before engaging in the conversation.

The Rewards of Active Listening

Stronger Relationships: Active listening builds trust, fosters intimacy, and strengthens relationships with friends, family, and loved ones.

Improved Communication: By truly listening to others, you can avoid misunderstandings and improve the overall quality of your communication.

Increased Empathy and Understanding: Active listening cultivates empathy and helps you to see the world from another person's perspective.

Enhanced Problem-Solving: When people feel heard and understood, they are more likely to be open to finding collaborative solutions.

Active listening is a valuable skill that can enrich all aspects of your life. By cultivating the art of truly listening, you can deepen your connections, improve your communication, and create a more understanding and compassionate world.

I hope this chapter provides you with valuable insights into the power of active listening. In the next chapter, we'll explore the role of body language in active listening and how it enhances the listening experience.

PPP

The Body Language of Listening: Speaking Volumes Without a Word

We often think of communication as solely about the words we speak. But the truth is, our bodies are constantly communicating, sending subtle messages that can either enhance or hinder our ability to connect with others. This is particularly true when it comes to active listening.

Body language is a powerful tool that can amplify or undermine our listening efforts. Imagine this: you're sharing a personal anecdote, and the other person is looking at their phone, crossing their arms, and sighing impatiently. How does that make you feel? Likely, it makes you feel unheard, unimportant, and perhaps even a little hurt.

The Language of the Body:

Open and Inviting: When we are truly listening, our body language reflects it. We tend to lean forward slightly, maintain open posture with uncrossed arms and legs, and make occasional nods to show that we're engaged.

Mirroring (Subtly): Unconsciously, we may subtly mirror the other person's body language, creating a sense of rapport and connection. This might involve mirroring their posture, their pace of speech, or even their subtle gestures.

Facial Expressions: Our facial expressions speak volumes. A genuine smile, a furrowed brow, or a look of concern can all convey our level of engagement and understanding.

The Importance of Nonverbal Cues:

Building Trust and Rapport: Open and inviting body language fosters trust and rapport. It signals to the speaker that you are genuinely interested in what they have to say.

Improving Empathy: By paying attention to the other person's body language, we can gain valuable insights into their emotions and perspectives.

Demonstrating Respect: Respectful body language shows that you value the speaker and their message. It communicates that you are present, attentive, and genuinely interested in what they have to say.

Common Listening Barriers (Body Language):

Closed-off Posture: Crossing your arms, slouching in your chair, or looking around the room can signal disinterest and disengagement.

Distracted Behavior: Checking your phone, fidgeting, or looking away frequently can make the speaker feel unheard and unimportant.

Impatience: Sighing, tapping your foot, or looking at the clock can convey impatience and disrespect.

Active listening is a multifaceted skill that encompasses both verbal and nonverbal communication. By paying attention to our own body language and interpreting the body language of others, we can enhance our listening skills, build stronger connections, and create a more meaningful and empathetic communication experience.

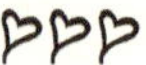

SEVEN

COMPLIMENT GENUINELY- IT OPENS HEARTS

You're walking down the street, minding your own business, when someone stops you and says, "I absolutely love your shoes! They're so unique." How does that make you feel? Chances are, it puts a smile on your face. You feel seen, appreciated, and maybe even a little bit special.

That's the magic of a genuine compliment. It's like a tiny spark of joy, a small act of kindness that can brighten someone's day and strengthen the bonds between us.

We all crave recognition. We want to feel valued, appreciated, and seen for who we are. A genuine compliment, delivered with sincerity and specificity, can be a powerful antidote to the negativity and self-doubt that we all experience from time to time.

ϼϼϼ

More Than Just "Nice Job": **The Art of the Meaningful Compliment**

Think beyond generic compliments like "Nice work!" or "You look good today." These can feel a bit hollow and insincere. Instead, try to offer specific and heartfelt compliments that highlight someone's unique qualities and achievements.

<u>Focus on Effort and Achievement</u>: Instead of saying "You're so talented," try "I was really impressed with the creativity and hard work you put into that presentation."

<u>Acknowledge Their Strengths</u>: Compliment someone's kindness, their empathy, their sense of humor, their dedication, or any other positive qualities you admire.

<u>Be Specific and Detailed</u>: Instead of saying "You're a great listener," try "I really appreciate how you always take the time to listen to my concerns and offer helpful advice."

<u>Offer Genuine Praise</u>: Let your words come from the heart. Avoid insincere flattery or compliments that feel forced.

ᗞᗞᗞ

The Ripple Effect of Genuine Appreciation

The impact of a genuine compliment can be far-reaching.

<u>Boosting Self-Esteem</u>: When someone receives a sincere compliment, it can significantly boost their self-esteem and confidence. It reinforces their positive qualities and reminds them of their value.

<u>Strengthening Relationships</u>: Genuine compliments foster positive relationships by creating a sense of warmth, appreciation, and connection. They build trust and strengthen the bonds between us.

<u>Creating a Positive Atmosphere</u>: When we offer and receive genuine compliments, we create a more positive and uplifting environment for ourselves and those around us.

<u>Encouraging Growth</u>: Genuine compliments can motivate and inspire others to strive for excellence. When someone feels appreciated for their efforts, they are more likely to continue to grow and develop.

ᗞᗞᗞ

Giving and Receiving Compliments Gracefully

<u>Accepting Compliments with Grace</u>: When someone compliments you, acknowledge it with a simple "Thank you" or "I appreciate that."

<u>Returning the Favor</u>: If someone compliments you, take a moment to return the favor. Offer a genuine compliment in response. This creates a positive and reciprocal exchange.

<u>Be Mindful of Cultural Differences</u>: Cultural norms around compliments can vary significantly. Be mindful of these differences and adjust your approach accordingly.

Genuine compliments are a powerful tool for building stronger relationships, boosting self-esteem, and creating a more positive and uplifting world. They are a small act of kindness that can have a profound impact on those around us.

So, let's make a conscious effort to offer more genuine compliments and to receive them with grace.

ppp

EIGHT

USE OPEN BODY LANGUAGE- CROSSED ARMS CAN CLOSE THE CONNECTION

We often think of communication as solely about the words we speak, but the truth is, our bodies are constantly speaking their own language. Our posture, gestures, and facial expressions all convey subtle messages that can significantly impact how others perceive us and how effectively we communicate.

The Power of Open Body Language

Inviting Connection: Open body language signals to others that you are approachable, receptive, and engaged. It creates a sense of openness and invites others to connect with you.

Building Trust and Rapport: When you maintain open posture, you subconsciously communicate trust and honesty. It makes the other person feel more comfortable and encourages them to open up and share their thoughts and feelings.

Enhancing Empathy: Open body language helps to foster empathy and understanding. When you mirror the other person's open posture, you create a sense of harmony and connection.

Projecting Confidence: Open posture can also boost your own confidence. Standing tall, making eye contact, and using open gestures can make you feel more assertive and empowered.

The Language of Closed-Off Body Language:

Creating Distance: Crossed arms, folded legs, and avoiding eye contact can create a sense of distance and disengagement. It can make the other person feel uncomfortable or unwelcome.

Signaling Disagreement or Discomfort: Crossed arms can sometimes be interpreted as a sign of defensiveness or disagreement.

Hindering Communication: Closed-off body language can create barriers to communication. It can make it more difficult for others to connect with you and understand your perspective.

ᗡᗡᗡ

Mastering the Art of Open Body Language:

Uncross Your Arms and Legs: Keep your arms and legs uncrossed. This signals openness and receptivity.

Lean Forward Slightly: Leaning forward slightly shows that you're engaged and interested in the conversation.

Maintain Open Posture: Keep your shoulders relaxed and your chest open. Avoid slouching or hunching over.

Use Gestures Mindfully: Use open and inviting gestures to emphasize your points and illustrate your ideas.

Mirror Open Body Language: If the other person is displaying open body language, subtly mirror their posture to create a sense of harmony and connection.

ᗡᗡᗡ

Self-Awareness: The Mirror to Your Communication

Imagine this: You're trying to have a serious conversation with a friend, but you find yourself unconsciously crossing your arms and avoiding eye contact. You might not even realize you're doing it, but your body language is sending a message of defensiveness or disinterest, even if your words are saying something completely different.

This highlights the crucial role of self-awareness in understanding and interpreting our own body language. Just as we strive to understand the nonverbal cues of others, we must also become more aware of the messages our own bodies are constantly transmitting.

Decoding Your Own Signals: Pay attention to your own body language. When you're feeling anxious, do you tend to fidget? When you're feeling confident, do you stand tall and make eye contact? Becoming aware of these patterns can help you understand how your body language reflects your inner state.

<u>Identifying Your Go-To Gestures</u>: We all have our own unique set of go-to gestures – a particular way of gesturing with our hands, a tendency to touch our face, or a nervous habit like tapping our foot. Recognizing these patterns can help you become more mindful of your body language and how it might be perceived by others.

<u>The Impact of Your Emotions</u>: Our emotions have a significant impact on our body language. When we're feeling stressed, our shoulders might tense up. When we're feeling excited, we might gesticulate more widely. Understanding this connection allows us to better manage our emotions and communicate more effectively.

<u>Using Body Language Intentionally</u>: Once you become more aware of your own body language, you can start to use it more intentionally. For example, if you want to appear more confident in a presentation, you can stand tall, make eye contact, and use open and confident gestures.

ᗪᗪᗪ

Self-Awareness: The Foundation for Authentic Communication

Understanding your own body language is not just about being aware of your physical movements; it's about understanding how your inner state is reflected in your outward expression. By becoming more self-aware, you can:

<u>Communicate More Authentically</u>: Your words and your body language will align more closely, creating a more genuine and authentic communication style.

<u>Build Stronger Relationships</u>: When you are aware of the messages your body is sending, you can ensure that your nonverbal communication is congruent with your intentions.

<u>Manage Stress and Anxiety</u>: By observing your own body language, you can become more aware of your stress levels and take steps to manage them effectively.

Body language is a powerful form of nonverbal communication. By cultivating open and inviting body language, we can create a more positive and engaging communication experience for ourselves and others. Remember, our bodies are constantly speaking, so let's make sure they're sending the right message.

ᗪᗪᗪ

NINE

SEND HANDWRITTEN NOTES OF APPRECIATION- IT'S A PERSONAL TOUCH

In our increasingly digital world, where communication often happens through fleeting texts and impersonal emails, the art of handwritten communication risks fading into obscurity. Yet, there's a unique magic to a handwritten note that transcends the speed and convenience of digital communication.

Imagine receiving a letter, not an email, from a friend or loved one. The feel of the paper, the unique slant of their handwriting, the faint scent of ink – these sensory details create a multi-sensory experience that instantly transports you back to a simpler time. It's a tangible reminder of human connection, a testament to the time and effort someone invested in reaching out to you.

ᐳᐳᐳ

More Than Just Words: The Power of the Written Word

A handwritten note is more than just a message; it's a tangible expression of thoughtfulness and care.

<u>A Touch of the Human Hand</u>: In our increasingly digital world, the act of handwriting itself is a unique and valuable skill. It involves a deliberate engagement of the mind and body, requiring focus and intention.

A Symbol of Sincere Effort: Taking the time to handwrite a note demonstrates a level of care and consideration that goes beyond a quickly typed email or text message. It shows the recipient that you value their time and that you've put genuine effort into expressing your thoughts.

A Lasting Impression: Handwritten notes have a way of staying with us long after they've been read. They become cherished keepsakes, tucked away in drawers or displayed on desks, serving as reminders of special moments and meaningful connections.

Boosting Morale: Whether it's a thank-you note, a note of encouragement, or simply a friendly hello, a handwritten note can brighten someone's day and boost their morale. It's a small act of kindness that can have a profound and lasting impact.

ppp

The Art of Crafting Meaningful Notes:

Choose the Right Stationery: Select high-quality stationery that reflects your personality and the occasion.

Write with Intention: Take your time and write with intention. Put your heart and soul into your words.

Personalize Your Message: Tailor your message to the recipient. Mention something specific you appreciate about them, share a personal anecdote, or express your gratitude for their presence in your life.

Add a Personal Touch: Consider adding a small drawing, a pressed flower, or a sprig of dried herbs to personalize your note even further.

Present it with Care: Hand-deliver the note whenever possible. If that's not feasible, choose a beautiful envelope and present it with care.

ppp

Rediscovering the Lost Art of Handwritten Communication

In our fast-paced digital world, taking the time to write a handwritten note can feel like a luxury. But the rewards are immeasurable. It's a way to reconnect with a simpler, more human way of communicating, to cultivate mindfulness and intentionality in our interactions, and to leave a lasting impression on those we care about.

So, the next time you want to express your gratitude, offer encouragement, or simply let someone know you're thinking of them, consider the power of a handwritten note. It may be a small gesture, but it can have a profound impact on the lives of those around you.

❧❧❧

TEN

FOLLOW UP AFTER MEETINGS- IT STRENGTHENS THE RELATIONSHIP

You've just wrapped up a productive meeting. You shook hands, exchanged pleasantries, and headed off to your next task. But wait! The meeting isn't truly over until you've followed up.

Think of a follow-up as the icing on the cake. It's that extra touch that solidifies the connection, demonstrates your commitment, and ensures that the outcomes of the meeting are actually achieved.

Why Follow-Up Matters:

<u>Reinforces Key Decisions</u>: A follow-up email or phone call provides a written record of the meeting's key decisions, action items, and next steps. This minimizes confusion and ensures everyone is on the same page.

<u>Demonstrates Professionalism</u>: Following up promptly and effectively demonstrates your professionalism, organization, and attention to detail.

<u>Strengthens Relationships</u>: It shows the other person that you value their time and that you're committed to moving the conversation forward.

<u>Increases Accountability</u>: By outlining next steps and deadlines, a follow-up helps ensure that everyone stays accountable and that the agreed-upon actions are completed.

ᑭᑭᑭ

The Art of the Effective Follow-Up:

Timeliness is Key: Aim to send a follow-up email within 24 hours of the meeting.

Keep it Concise and Clear: Summarize the key takeaways, action items, and deadlines in a concise and easy-to-read format.

Personalize Your Message: Tailor your message to the specific individuals and the context of the meeting.

Use a Professional Tone: Maintain a professional and courteous tone throughout your communication.

Encourage Feedback: Encourage the recipient to provide feedback or ask any clarifying questions.

Example Follow-Up Email:

Subject: Following Up - [Meeting Topic]

Dear [Name],

It was a pleasure meeting with you today to discuss [briefly state the meeting topic].

Here are the key takeaways from our conversation:

Action Item 1: [Action item 1] - [Deadline]

Action Item 2: [Action Item 2] - [Deadline]

Please let me know if you have any questions or require any further information.

Thank you again for your time and valuable insights.

Sincerely,

[Your Name]

**Exercise:

**Imagine you just had a meeting with a potential client to discuss a marketing proposal. Write a sample follow-up email based on the following:

Key Takeaways:

Client agreed to the proposed budget.

Next steps: Schedule a kickoff meeting to discuss project timelines and deliverables.

Client requested a sample social media post before making a final decision.

The Power of the Follow-Up: A Small Gesture with Big Impact

Following up may seem like a small gesture, but it can have a significant impact on your relationships and your success. It demonstrates your professionalism, reinforces your commitment, and strengthens your connections with others. So, the next time you have a meeting, remember the power of the follow-up. It's a small investment of time that can yield significant returns.

Remember:

Follow-up is a crucial step in any successful interaction.

Keep your follow-up emails concise, clear, and professional.

Personalize your messages to create a stronger impact.

Use follow-ups to reinforce key decisions and ensure accountability.

By incorporating these tips into your communication style, you can strengthen your relationships, increase your productivity, and achieve greater success in all your endeavors.

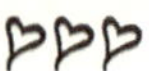

ELEVEN

REMEMBER IMPORTANT DATES—IT SHOWS YOU CARE

Let's be honest, remembering birthdays, anniversaries, and other important dates can feel like a Herculean task. Our minds are constantly bombarded with information, and keeping track of all those special days can feel like trying to juggle a dozen watermelons. But trust me, the effort is worth it.

The Power of Remembering:

<u>Strengthening Relationships</u>: Remembering important dates shows that you care. It demonstrates that you pay attention, that you value your relationships, and that you're willing to go the extra mile.

<u>Building Trust and Intimacy</u>: When you remember a friend's birthday or your partner's anniversary, it shows you're thoughtful and considerate. This builds trust and strengthens your bond.

<u>Avoiding Awkward Situations</u>: Forgetting a significant date, like a birthday or anniversary, can lead to awkward situations and hurt feelings. Let's face it, nobody wants to be the one who forgot their partner's birthday!

<u>Showing Appreciation</u>: Remembering important dates is a simple yet powerful way to show your appreciation for the people in your life. It's a small gesture that can have a big impact.

♡♡♡

Tips for Remembering Important Dates:

<u>The Calendar is Your Best Friend</u>:

Invest in a good calendar – physical or digital – and use it religiously.

Set reminders on your phone, computer, or even your smartwatch.

Use a calendar app that allows you to set recurring reminders for birthdays and anniversaries.

The "Birthday Buddy" System: Team up with a friend or family member to exchange birthday reminders.

The "Birthday Basket" Trick: Keep a small basket or box where you jot down important dates throughout the year.

The "Memory Palace" Technique: This ancient memory technique involves associating dates with vivid mental images. For example, if your friend's birthday is on July 4th, imagine them celebrating their birthday with a spectacular fireworks display.

Fun Ways to Celebrate:

Go the Extra Mile: Instead of just sending a generic birthday message, consider sending a handwritten card, baking a cake, or planning a surprise outing.

Personalized Gifts: Choose gifts that are thoughtful and personalized.

Celebrate Together: Plan a special celebration to commemorate the occasion.

ᐅᐅᐅ

Remembering Important Dates: A Lifelong Skill

Remembering important dates is a valuable life skill that strengthens relationships and demonstrates thoughtfulness and consideration. By incorporating these tips and tricks into your daily routine, you can ensure that you never forget a special occasion.

Reflection Questions:

What are some of the most important dates in your life?

How do you currently keep track of important dates?

What strategies can you implement to improve your memory of important dates?

Remember: Remembering important dates is not just about avoiding awkward situations; it's about showing the people you care about that they are valued and cherished. So, make an effort to remember those special days, and watch your relationships flourish.

ᐅᐅᐅ

TWELVE

PRACTICE GRATITUDE OFTEN—IT DEEPENS BONDS

In our fast-paced world, it's easy to get caught up in the hustle and bustle and forget to appreciate the good things in our lives. We often take for granted the simple joys – a warm sunny day, a delicious cup of coffee, the laughter of loved ones. But what if we shifted our focus? What if we took a moment each day to simply appreciate?

Practicing gratitude is more than just saying "thank you." It's about cultivating an attitude of appreciation and recognizing the abundance in our lives.

The Magic of Gratitude:

A Mood Booster: Studies have shown that practicing gratitude can significantly boost your mood. When you focus on the positive aspects of your life, you shift your perspective from scarcity to abundance, leading to increased happiness and overall well-being.

Strengthened Relationships: Expressing gratitude to others strengthens your bonds. A simple "thank you" can go a long way in showing your appreciation for their kindness, support, and friendship.

Reduced Stress and Anxiety: Focusing on gratitude helps to shift your attention away from worries and anxieties. It allows you to appreciate the present moment and find joy in the simple things.

Increased Compassion and Empathy: Practicing gratitude can increase your empathy and compassion for others. When you appreciate the good in your own life, you're more likely to recognize and appreciate the good in others.

ᐅᐅᐅ

Simple Ways to Cultivate Gratitude:

<u>Gratitude Journaling</u>: Dedicate a few minutes each day to writing down three things you're grateful for. It could be anything from a delicious meal to a kind gesture from a stranger.

<u>Expressing Gratitude Out Loud</u>: Tell your loved ones how much you appreciate them. Thank your partner for a delicious meal, your children for their laughter, and your friends for their support.

<u>Mindful Appreciation</u>: Take time to savor and appreciate the simple pleasures in life. Notice the beauty of a sunset, the taste of your favorite food, the feeling of sunshine on your skin.

<u>Acts of Kindness</u>: Expressing gratitude through acts of kindness, such as volunteering your time or helping a neighbor, can deepen your sense of appreciation and connection.

ᐅᐅᐅ

Fun Gratitude Exercises:

<u>"Three Good Things" Jar</u>: Every evening, write down three good things that happened that day on a piece of paper and put it in a jar. On a rainy day or when you're feeling down, open the jar and read through the notes.

<u>"Gratitude Walks"</u>: Take a walk and consciously notice the beauty around you – the trees, the flowers, the birdsong.

<u>"Gratitude Dinner"</u>: At dinner, go around the table and have each family member share one thing they are grateful for that day.

What are three things you are grateful for today?

How can you express your gratitude to someone you care about today?

How does practicing gratitude make you feel?

By cultivating a daily practice of gratitude, you can shift your perspective, enhance your well-being, and strengthen your connections with the people around you. So, let's make gratitude a daily habit and experience the transformative power of appreciation.

ᐅᐅᐅ

THIRTEEN

SHARE A LAUGH—IT BUILDS A SENSE OF CAMARADERIE

Laughter is truly the best medicine. It's contagious, it's uplifting, and it has the magical ability to bring people together. Sharing a laugh with others is more than just a fun pastime; it's a powerful tool for building stronger relationships, reducing stress, and creating a more positive and enjoyable experience for everyone involved.

The Science of Laughter:

Stress Buster: When we laugh, our bodies release endorphins, natural mood boosters that have stress-reducing effects. Laughter can also help to lower blood pressure and boost the immune system.

Connection Catalyst: Shared laughter creates a sense of camaraderie and connection. It fosters a feeling of belonging and strengthens the bonds between individuals.

Emotional Release: Laughter can help to release pent-up emotions, such as anger, frustration, and anxiety. It provides a healthy outlet for stress and allows us to feel lighter and more relaxed.

Improved Mood: Laughter is a mood booster. It can help to improve our mood, increase our energy levels, and enhance our overall sense of well-being.

ᑭᑭᑭ

Finding Humor in Everyday Life:

<u>Embrace the Absurd</u>: Find humor in the everyday – the silly things we do, the unexpected situations we encounter, and the quirks of human nature.

<u>Share Jokes and Funny Stories</u>: Tell jokes, share funny anecdotes, and enjoy a good laugh with friends and family.

<u>Watch Funny Movies and TV Shows</u>: Enjoy a good comedy movie or TV show with friends.

<u>Play Games</u>: Games like charades, Pictionary, and board games often involve humor and laughter.

<u>Find Humor in Yourself</u>: Don't be afraid to laugh at yourself. Self-deprecating humor (in moderation) can be a great way to connect with others and lighten the mood.

<u>Laughter Yoga</u>: A Fun Exercise

<u>Find a Laughter Yoga group</u>: These groups often incorporate simple laughter exercises and playful games to encourage laughter and social connection.

<u>Practice "fake" laughter</u>: Even if you don't feel like laughing initially, try forcing a laugh. You might be surprised at how quickly it becomes genuine.

What makes you laugh?

How often do you share laughter with others?

How does laughter make you feel?

Laughter is truly contagious. It's a simple yet powerful tool that can bring people together, reduce stress, and enhance our overall well-being. So, let's embrace the power of laughter, share our joy with others, and create a more lighthearted and enjoyable experience for ourselves and those around us.

Remember: Laughter is the best medicine!

ᑫᑫᑫ

FOURTEEN

BE PUNCTUAL—IT SHOWS RESPECT FOR OTHERS' TIME

We've all been there. You're running late for a meeting, frantically searching for your keys, and apologizing profusely as you burst through the door. While we all have those occasional "oops" moments, being consistently late can have a significant impact on our relationships and our overall success.

The Power of Punctuality:

Respect for Others' Time: Being punctual shows that you value other people's time and that you respect their commitments.

Building Trust and Reliability: When you're consistently on time, you build a reputation for reliability and trustworthiness.

Increased Productivity: Punctuality leads to smoother meetings, improved workflow, and increased productivity.

Reduced Stress: Arriving late often leads to feelings of stress and anxiety. Being punctual helps you feel more relaxed and in control.

ᗞᗞᗞ

Tips for Improving Your Punctuality:

Plan Ahead:

"The Two-Minute Rule": Always plan to arrive at least two minutes early. This gives you a buffer in case of unexpected delays.

Map Your Route: If you're unfamiliar with the location, map out your route beforehand to account for potential traffic delays.

<u>Prepare in Advance</u>: Gather your belongings, check your appearance, and double-check any necessary documents before you leave the house.

𝔭𝔭𝔭

Time Management Techniques:

<u>The Eisenhower Matrix</u>: Prioritize tasks and allocate time effectively.

<u>The Pomodoro Technique</u>: Work in focused bursts with short breaks to improve productivity and avoid procrastination.

<u>Embrace the "Early Bird" Mentality</u>: Aim to arrive a few minutes early for appointments and meetings. This allows you to settle in, gather your thoughts, and make a good first impression.

𝔭𝔭𝔭

Fun Fact:

Did you know that punctuality is highly valued in many cultures? In some cultures, being late can be considered a serious social faux pas.

Reflection Questions:

What are your biggest time-wasters?

How can you improve your time management skills?

What are the consequences of being consistently late?

How does punctuality impact your relationships and your overall success?

Actionable Insights:

Set reminders for important appointments.

**Plan your day in advance and allocate sufficient time for travel.

Practice good time management techniques.

Make a conscious effort to be on time for all your commitments.

By cultivating a culture of punctuality, we demonstrate respect for ourselves and others, improve our productivity, and create a more efficient and enjoyable experience for everyone involved.

𝔭𝔭𝔭

FIFTEEN

STAY CURIOUS—ASK THOUGHTFUL QUESTIONS TO SHOW INTEREST

Imagine you're at a party, and someone starts telling you about their amazing trip to Machu Picchu. Do you just nod and say, "That sounds cool," and move on? Or do you ask follow-up questions like, "What was the most challenging part of the hike?" or "What was the most memorable thing you saw?"

The latter approach not only shows genuine interest but also deepens the conversation and makes the other person feel valued and heard.

The Power of Curious Questions:

<u>Building Deeper Connections:</u> Thoughtful questions go beyond surface-level conversation. They encourage the other person to open up, share their thoughts and feelings, and connect with you on a deeper level.

<u>Demonstrating Genuine Interest:</u> Asking insightful questions shows that you're truly interested in the other person and what they have to say. It makes them feel valued and appreciated.

<u>Learning and Growth:</u> By asking thoughtful questions, you're not only learning about the other person, but you're also expanding your own knowledge and broadening your horizons.

<u>Fostering Creativity and Innovation:</u> When you ask "why?" and "what if?" questions, you encourage creative thinking and stimulate new ideas.

ᗷᗷᗷ

The Art of Asking Insightful Questions:

Go Beyond the Obvious: Avoid asking generic questions like "How are you?" or "What do you do for a living?" Instead, try asking more specific and engaging questions.

Listen Actively: Pay close attention to what the other person is saying. Listen not just to the words, but also to their tone of voice, their body language, and the emotions they convey.

Use Open-Ended Questions: Open-ended questions, which begin with "What," "How," "Why," "Tell me more about..." encourage the other person to elaborate and share their thoughts more fully.

Follow Their Lead: Let the conversation guide your questions. Build upon the other person's responses and explore their interests further.

Fun Question Games:

"20 Questions": This classic game is a fun way to practice asking insightful questions.

"Never Have I Ever" (with a twist): Instead of focusing on embarrassing situations, ask "Never Have I Ever" questions that encourage deeper conversations. For example, "Never have I ever traveled to another country."

What are some of your favorite questions to ask others?

How can you improve your questioning skills?

How do you feel when someone asks you insightful questions?

Asking thoughtful questions is a powerful tool for building stronger relationships, fostering deeper connections, and expanding your own knowledge and understanding of the world. So, the next time you're in conversation, remember to be curious, to listen attentively, and to ask questions that truly engage and inspire.

ᗷᗷᗷ

SIXTEEN

OFFER HELP WITHOUT BEING ASKED—IT BUILDS GOODWILL

Have you ever been in a situation where you needed a hand, and just when you were about to ask, someone stepped up and offered to help? That feeling of relief, of being seen and supported, is truly something special.

Offering help without being asked isn't just about being nice – it's about building stronger connections, creating a ripple effect of kindness, and making the world a slightly better place.

The Unexpected Helper: A Superhero in Disguise

Imagine this: You're struggling to carry a stack of heavy books to your car. Suddenly, a stranger appears, asking, "Need a hand with those?" That unexpected act of kindness can brighten your day and restore your faith in humanity.

Building Stronger Connections: When you offer help without being asked, you're showing the other person that you care. It fosters a sense of connection and builds goodwill.

Creating a Ripple Effect: Acts of kindness have a ripple effect. When you help someone, they are more likely to help others in need, creating a chain reaction of generosity.

Boosting Your Own Mood: Helping others can give you a sense of purpose and fulfillment. It can boost your mood and increase your overall well-being.

Cultivating a Culture of Kindness: By offering unsolicited help, you contribute to a culture of kindness and compassion. You inspire others to be more mindful of the needs of those around them.

PPP

Finding Opportunities to Be a "Unexpected Helper":

Be Observant: Pay attention to your surroundings. Who might need a helping hand? An elderly person struggling with groceries, a parent juggling a stroller and a toddler, a colleague looking overwhelmed with work.

The "Random Acts of Kindness" Challenge: Challenge yourself to perform one random act of kindness each day. It could be as simple as holding the door open for someone, offering to help a colleague with a task, or leaving a positive note for a friend.

Volunteer Your Time: Volunteer at a local shelter, help out at a community garden, or mentor a young person.

Offer a Listening Ear: Sometimes the greatest help we can offer is simply to listen. If you notice a friend or family member seems upset, offer a listening ear and a shoulder to lean on.

Fun Fact: Studies have shown that acts of kindness can actually increase your own happiness and well-being. So, by helping others, you're not only making their day better, but also improving your own mood!

PPP

Reflection Questions:

When was the last time someone offered you help without being asked? How did it make you feel?

What are some ways you can incorporate more acts of kindness into your daily routine?

How can you encourage others to be more helpful and compassionate?

Being an "unexpected helper" is a powerful way to make a positive impact on the world. It's a reminder that even small acts of kindness can have a profound effect on others and create a ripple effect of generosity.

So, the next time you see an opportunity to help, don't hesitate to lend a hand. You might be surprised at the positive impact you can make.

PPP

SEVENTEEN

RESPECT CULTURAL DIFFERENCES—IT DEMONSTRATES UNDERSTANDING

Imagine walking into a room full of people from different backgrounds. It's like stepping into a vibrant tapestry woven with a thousand different threads – a tapestry of cultures, traditions, and perspectives. This diversity enriches our lives and makes the world a more interesting place. However, navigating this diverse landscape requires a crucial ingredient: respect for cultural differences.

Why Respecting Cultural Differences Matters:

<u>Fostering Understanding and Tolerance</u>: When we respect cultural differences, we break down barriers, reduce prejudice, and foster a more inclusive and tolerant society.

<u>Building Stronger Relationships</u>: Respecting and valuing the cultural backgrounds of others strengthens our relationships with friends, colleagues, and community members.

<u>Enhancing Communication</u>: Understanding and respecting cultural differences improves our communication skills, allowing us to connect with people from diverse backgrounds more effectively.

<u>Promoting Innovation and Creativity</u>: Exposure to different cultures can broaden our horizons, challenge our assumptions, and spark new ideas and perspectives.

ᗡᗡᗡ

Tips for Respecting Cultural Differences:

<u>Be Curious and Inquisitive</u>: Ask questions about other cultures with genuine interest. Be open to learning about different customs, traditions, and perspectives.

<u>Practice Active Listening</u>: When interacting with people from different cultures, actively listen to their perspectives and try to understand their point of view, even if it differs from your own.

<u>Be Mindful of Your Own Biases</u>: We all have unconscious biases. Be aware of your own biases and actively work to overcome them.

<u>Learn Basic Cultural Etiquette</u>: Research basic cultural etiquette, such as appropriate greetings, dining etiquette, and gift-giving customs.

<u>Embrace Diversity</u>: Celebrate the richness and diversity of human cultures. Embrace opportunities to learn from and interact with people from different backgrounds.

<u>Fun Fact</u>: *Did you know that there are over 7,000 languages spoken around the world? This incredible diversity reflects the richness and complexity of human culture.*

Reflection Questions:

What are some of the cultural differences you've encountered in your own life?

How can you be more mindful of cultural differences in your daily interactions?

How can you use your own cultural background to enrich the lives of others?

Respecting cultural differences is not just about being polite; it's about embracing the richness and diversity of the human experience. By cultivating an attitude of curiosity, empathy, and respect, we can build bridges of understanding and create a more inclusive and harmonious world.

Remember: Every culture has its own unique beauty and value. Let's celebrate our differences and learn from each other.

ᗡᗡᗡ

EIGHTEEN

SHARE YOUR AUTHENTIC SELF—IT FOSTERS TRUST

Imagine walking into a room and feeling like you have to put on a mask – pretending to be someone you're not, suppressing your true self to fit in. Exhausting, right?

Authenticity, on the other hand, is like a breath of fresh air. It's about being true to yourself, embracing your unique quirks and qualities, and expressing your genuine thoughts and feelings.

The Magic of Being Yourself:

Building Trust and Intimacy: When you're authentic, you create a sense of trust and intimacy in your relationships. People are drawn to those who are genuine and genuine people attract others who are genuine.

Reduced Stress and Anxiety: Trying to be someone you're not is exhausting! Authenticity frees you from the constant pressure to conform and allows you to relax and be yourself.

Increased Self-Confidence: Embracing your true self boosts your self-esteem and confidence. You feel more comfortable in your own skin and more empowered to live your life on your own terms.

Fostering Creativity and Innovation: When you're not worried about fitting in, you're more likely to be creative, innovative, and express your unique talents and perspectives.

Tips for Embracing Your Authentic Self:

<u>Identify Your Values</u>: What truly matters to you? What are your core values?

<u>Recognize Your Strengths and Weaknesses</u>: Understand your strengths and weaknesses without judgment.

<u>Set Boundaries</u>: Learn to say "no" to things that don't align with your values.

<u>Express Your Opinions Honestly</u>: Share your thoughts and feelings authentically, even if it means going against the grain.

<u>Embrace Your Quirks</u>: Don't try to be someone you're not. Embrace your unique quirks and personality traits.

Fun Fact: Studies have shown that people who are authentic in their relationships tend to experience higher levels of life satisfaction and well-being.

What are some ways in which you might be trying to be someone you're not?

What are your core values? How can you live more authentically in alignment with those values?

What would it feel like to truly embrace your authentic self?

Authenticity is not about being perfect; it's about being real. It's about embracing your unique strengths and weaknesses, expressing your true self, and living a life that reflects your values and beliefs.

By embracing your authenticity, you can build stronger relationships, increase your self-confidence, and live a more fulfilling and meaningful life.

So, take a deep breath, embrace your true colors, and let your authentic self shine!

ᐅᐅᐅ

NINETEEN

USE STORIES TO CONNECT EMOTIONALLY—IT MAKES YOU RELATABLE

Alright, let's get real for a moment. Have you ever been in a conversation where you feel like you're just exchanging pleasantries, like two ships passing in the night? You know, the kind where you ask "How are you?" and they reply "Good, and you?" and then you're both left wondering what to talk about next.

Well, my friend, I'm here to introduce you to a secret weapon: the power of storytelling.

Think about it. Stories are woven into the fabric of our existence. From ancient myths and legends to the bedtime stories we tell our children, stories have the incredible ability to connect us on a deeper level.

Why Stories Matter:

Break Down Walls: Stories have a magical way of breaking down barriers. When you share a personal anecdote, you're opening a window into your soul, inviting others to glimpse your joys, sorrows, and unique perspective.

<u>Build Empathy and Understanding</u>: By sharing your experiences, you allow others to step into your shoes, to feel what you felt, and to understand your point of view. This fosters empathy and creates a deeper level of connection.

Make Complex Ideas Memorable: Let's face it, dry facts can be a bit...well, dry. But when you wrap those facts in a compelling story, they come alive. Stories make information more engaging, memorable, and easier to understand.

Inspire and Motivate: Stories have the power to inspire and motivate. They can teach us valuable lessons, show us that anything is possible, and give us the courage to pursue our dreams.

$$\wp\wp\wp$$

Unlocking Your Inner Storyteller:

Find Your Stories: Reflect on your life experiences. What are some of your most memorable moments? What lessons have you learned along the way?

Practice Sharing Your Stories: Start with small steps. Share a quick anecdote with a friend over coffee, or tell a story to your family at dinner.

Become a Master Listener: Pay close attention to the stories of others. Ask follow-up questions, show genuine interest, and let them know that you value their experiences.

Use Stories to Illustrate Your Points: When communicating your ideas, use stories to bring your message to life. For example, instead of simply stating a fact, share a personal experience that illustrates that point.

$$\wp\wp\wp$$

A Storytelling Exercise:

Think of a time when you overcame a challenge, learned a valuable lesson, or experienced a moment of pure joy. Now, try to tell that story to a friend or family member. Pay attention to their reactions. How does your story make them feel? What questions do they ask?

Stories are the threads that weave the tapestry of our lives. They connect us to each other, to our past, and to our shared humanity. So, embrace the power of storytelling, share your own unique experiences, and let your stories inspire and connect.

Now, go forth and share your tales with the world! I'm off to find a good book and get lost in a captivating story myself.

$$\wp\wp\wp$$

TWENTY

BE PRESENT—GIVE YOUR UNDIVIDED ATTENTION

In today's hyper-connected world, it's easy to get distracted. Our phones ping, notifications chime, and our minds race from one thought to the next. But what if I told you that giving your full attention – truly being present – is one of the most valuable gifts you can offer?

Think about it. Have you ever been in a conversation where you felt truly heard and understood? It's a powerful feeling, isn't it? When someone truly listens to you, you feel valued, respected, and connected.

The Magic of Presence:

<u>Deeper Connections</u>: When you give your undivided attention, you create a deeper sense of connection with the other person. They feel heard, valued, and understood, which strengthens your bond.

<u>Improved Communication</u>: Active listening fosters clearer communication. You're more likely to understand the other person's perspective, avoid misunderstandings, and respond thoughtfully.

<u>Reduced Stress</u>: Being present in the moment helps to reduce stress and anxiety. It allows you to savor the present moment and appreciate the beauty of the here and now.

<u>Increased Empathy and Understanding</u>: When you truly listen to others, you gain a deeper understanding of their perspectives and experiences. This cultivates empathy and compassion.

ϷϷϷ

Cultivating Presence in Your Daily Life:

<u>Mindful Moments</u>: Throughout the day, take a few moments to simply be present. Notice the sounds around you, the feeling of the sun on your skin, the taste of your food.

<u>Digital Detox</u>: Take breaks from your phone and other electronic devices. Schedule "no-phone" zones and times to disconnect and reconnect with the present moment.

<u>Practice Active Listening</u>: When someone is speaking, truly listen to what they are saying. Put away distractions, make eye contact, and reflect on their words.

<u>Embrace Boredom</u>: In our hyper-stimulated world, boredom can feel uncomfortable. But boredom can also be an opportunity for creativity, reflection, and inner peace.

ppp

A Fun Exercise: The "Mindful Listening Challenge"

For one day, make a conscious effort to truly listen to everyone you interact with. Put away your phone, make eye contact, and truly engage in the conversation. Notice how it changes your interactions and how others respond to your presence.

In a world that constantly demands our attention, the ability to be present is a rare and valuable gift. By cultivating mindfulness and practicing active listening, we can deepen our connections with others, enhance our well-being, and truly savor the richness of the present moment.

So, the next time you're in conversation, put away your distractions, truly listen, and experience the magic of being present.

ppp

TWENTY-ONE

LEARN AND REMEMBER PERSONAL DETAILS—IT STRENGTHENS RAPPORT

Let's be honest, remembering names can be a real struggle, especially when you meet a lot of new people. You shake hands, exchange pleasantries, and then poof, their name vanishes from your memory like a magician's disappearing act. But what if I told you that remembering names and other personal details is more than just a social grace – it's a powerful tool for building stronger relationships?

The Power of Personalization:

Imagine this: You're at a networking event, and you meet someone you met briefly at a conference months ago. Instead of awkwardly fumbling for their name, you greet them with a warm smile and say, "Hi [Name], it's so good to see you again! I was just thinking about our conversation about [shared interest] at the conference."

Now that's impressive!

<u>Building Rapport</u>: Remembering someone's name and other personal details shows that you pay attention, that you value them as an individual, and that you've taken the time to remember your interactions.

<u>Fostering Trust and Connection</u>: When you show genuine interest in someone by remembering their name and other details, it builds trust and fosters a deeper connection.

<u>Creating a Positive Impression</u>: Remembering names and details makes a strong positive impression. People appreciate being remembered and valued.

<u>Improving Your Communication</u>: Remembering personal details allows you to tailor your conversations, making them more relevant and engaging.

ᐡᐡᐡ

Tips for Remembering Names and Details:

The <u>"Name Game"</u>: When you meet someone new, repeat their name immediately. For example, "Nice to meet you, [Name]."

<u>Create Mental Associations</u>: Associate their name with a memorable characteristic, a physical feature, or something they mentioned during the conversation.

<u>Use Mnemonic Devices</u>: Try using memory techniques like the method of loci (associating names with locations) to improve your memory.

<u>Practice, Practice, Practice</u>: The more you practice remembering names, the better you'll become at it.

ᐡᐡᐡ

Fun Fact:

Did you know that remembering names is a sign of respect and intelligence across many cultures?

How good are you at remembering names?

What strategies can you implement to improve your memory for names and other personal details?

How can remembering personal details help you build stronger relationships?

Remembering names and other personal details may seem like a small gesture, but it can have a significant impact on your relationships. By making a conscious effort to remember the names and details of the people you meet, you can build stronger connections, foster deeper relationships, and make a lasting positive impression.

So, the next time you meet someone new, pay attention, make an effort to remember their name, and watch your relationships flourish.

ᐡᐡᐡ

TWENTY-TWO

SHOW PATIENCE—IT ENCOURAGES OPEN DIALOGUE

Patience is a Virtue (and a Communication Superpower!)

Let's face it, in our fast-paced world, patience can feel like a rare and endangered species. We're constantly bombarded with instant gratification – instant messaging, instant coffee, instant results. But in the realm of communication, patience is not just a virtue; it's a superpower!

Imagine trying to have a conversation with someone who's constantly interrupting you, eager to jump in with their own thoughts before you've even finished speaking. Frustrating, right? Patience, on the other hand, creates space for genuine dialogue, allowing everyone to fully express themselves and truly be heard.

The Magic of Patience in Communication:

Fostering Deeper Connections: When you patiently listen to others, you show them that you value their opinions and perspectives. This builds trust and fosters deeper connections.

Reducing Conflict: Patience helps to diffuse tense situations. When you give others the space to express themselves without interruption, you're less likely to misunderstand each other and more likely to find common ground.

Improving Communication Flow: Patience allows for a smoother and more natural flow of conversation. It gives everyone the time and space to formulate their thoughts and express themselves clearly.

<u>Cultivating Empathy</u>: By patiently listening to others, you gain a deeper understanding of their perspectives and experiences. This cultivates empathy and helps you to connect with others on a more human level.

ᛈᛈᛈ

Tips for Cultivating Patience in Communication:

<u>Practice Active Listening</u>: Truly listen to what the other person is saying, without interrupting or planning your response.

<u>Count to Five</u>: If you feel yourself getting impatient, take a deep breath and count to five before responding.

<u>Embrace the Pause</u>: Allow for moments of silence in the conversation. These pauses can actually enhance communication by giving everyone time to reflect and formulate their thoughts.

<u>Remember, everyone communicates differently</u>: Some people are naturally more thoughtful and deliberate in their speech. Be patient and understanding of different communication styles.

Fun Fact: *Did you know that some cultures place a high value on silence and consider it a form of communication?*

Reflection Time:

When are you most likely to lose patience in a conversation?

What are some strategies you can use to cultivate more patience in your communication?

How does patience contribute to your overall well-being?

Patience is not just about waiting; it's about creating space for understanding, empathy, and meaningful connection. By cultivating patience in our communication, we can build stronger relationships, resolve conflicts more effectively, and create a more harmonious and understanding world.

So, the next time you're in conversation, take a deep breath, be patient, and allow the conversation to unfold naturally. You might be surprised at the profound impact it can have.

ᛈᛈᛈ

TWENTY-THREE
ACKNOWLEDGE OTHERS' PERSPECTIVES—IT SHOWS RESPECT

Walking in Another's Shoes: The Power of Acknowledging Perspectives

Okay, let's be honest, we all have those moments. You're passionately debating a topic with a friend, and you're so sure you're right that you barely even listen to their point of view. We've all been there! But what if I told you that acknowledging other perspectives isn't just about being polite, it's actually a superpower for building stronger relationships and fostering a deeper understanding of the world?

Think of it this way: Imagine you're trying to assemble a puzzle. If you only look at the pieces from your own angle, you might miss the bigger picture. But if you step back, turn the puzzle around, and consider how the pieces fit together from different perspectives, you're much more likely to complete it successfully.

The Magic of Acknowledging Other Viewpoints:

<u>Building Bridges of Understanding:</u> When you acknowledge and respect other perspectives, you build bridges of understanding between yourself and others. You create a safe space for open dialogue and encourage others to share their own unique viewpoints.

<u>Fostering Empathy and Compassion:</u> By stepping into someone else's shoes and trying to see the world from their perspective, you cultivate

empathy and compassion. You begin to understand their motivations, their fears, and their hopes and dreams.

Expanding Your Horizons: Acknowledging other perspectives challenges your own assumptions and beliefs. It opens your mind to new ideas and helps you to broaden your understanding of the world.

Resolving Conflicts Peacefully: When you acknowledge and respect differing viewpoints, you're more likely to find common ground and resolve conflicts peacefully.

ᛯᛯᛯ

Tips for Acknowledging Other Perspectives:

Active Listening 101: Truly listen to what others have to say, without interrupting or planning your response.

"I" Statements: Use "I" statements to express your own perspective while acknowledging the other person's viewpoint. For example, instead of saying "You're wrong," try saying, "I understand your point of view, but I see it differently because..."

Seek Out Diverse Perspectives: Intentionally seek out and engage with people from different backgrounds and with different viewpoints.

Challenge Your Own Assumptions: Regularly question your own beliefs and assumptions. Are you holding onto any biases that are preventing you from seeing the bigger picture?

ᛯᛯᛯ

A Fun Exercise: "The Perspective Swap"

Choose a current event or a controversial topic. Try to see the situation from the perspective of someone who holds a different viewpoint. How does this shift in perspective change your understanding of the issue?

Acknowledging other perspectives is not just about being polite; it's about cultivating a deeper understanding of the world and building stronger, more meaningful connections with others.

So, the next time you engage in a conversation, remember to listen with an open mind, acknowledge different viewpoints, and embrace the richness of diverse perspectives.

You might be surprised at what you learn!

ᛯᛯᛯ

TWENTY-FOUR

BUILD A SENSE OF BELONGING—IT MAKES PEOPLE FEEL VALUED

Finding Your Tribe: The Importance of Belonging

Have you ever felt like you don't quite fit in? Like you're searching for a place where you truly belong? You're not alone! The human desire to belong is deeply ingrained within us. It's a fundamental need, like the need for food or water.

Think of it like this: Imagine yourself as a lone tree standing in a barren desert. Life would be tough, wouldn't it? But when you're surrounded by a forest of trees, you find shelter, support, and a sense of community.

The Magic of Belonging:

<u>A Boost for Well-being</u>: Feeling like you belong has a profound impact on your mental and emotional well-being. It reduces stress, boosts self-esteem, and increases your overall happiness.

<u>A Source of Support</u>: When you feel like you belong, you have a support system to lean on during challenging times. You know you have people in your corner who will offer a helping hand, a listening ear, and a shoulder to lean on.

<u>Fostering Creativity and Growth</u>: Feeling like you belong encourages you to be yourself, to express your unique talents and perspectives. It creates a safe and supportive environment for personal and professional growth.

<u>Building Stronger Communities</u>: When we all feel like we belong, we create stronger, more compassionate, and more inclusive communities.

ÞÞÞ

Cultivating a Sense of Belonging:

Join Groups and Communities: Find groups and communities that align with your interests and values. Whether it's a book club, a sports team, a volunteer organization, or a local community group, find your tribe!

Connect with Others: Make an effort to connect with people who share your interests and values. Strike up conversations with your neighbors, join a local club, or attend community events.

Volunteer Your Time: Volunteering is a fantastic way to connect with others and contribute to something meaningful.

Embrace Diversity: Celebrate the unique qualities that make each individual special. Embrace differences and learn from the diverse perspectives of those around you.

ÞÞÞ

Fun Fact: *Research has shown that a strong sense of belonging is associated with better physical health, increased longevity, and greater overall well-being.*

Reflection Questions:

Where do you feel a strong sense of belonging?

What can you do to cultivate a stronger sense of belonging in your life?

How can you help others feel like they belong?

The human desire to belong is deeply ingrained within us all. By actively seeking out connections, embracing diversity, and creating a sense of belonging for ourselves and others, we can build stronger communities, enhance our well-being, and create a more inclusive and compassionate world.

So, go out there and find your tribe! You belong.

ÞÞÞ

TWENTY-FIVE

MAINTAIN A POSITIVE TONE—IT MAKES INTERACTIONS UPLIFTING

The Power of Positivity: How a Sunny Disposition Brightens Every Interaction

Imagine this: You're having a conversation, and instead of focusing on the challenges, you highlight the opportunities. Instead of dwelling on the negatives, you focus on the positive aspects of the situation. Sounds like a recipe for a more enjoyable and uplifting experience, doesn't it?

Maintaining a positive tone in your communication is like adding a sprinkle of sunshine to every interaction. It creates a more pleasant atmosphere, fosters stronger relationships, and makes the world a little brighter for everyone involved.

The Magic of a Positive Vibe:

Attracts Positive Energy: Just like attracts like. When you radiate positivity, you attract positive people and experiences into your life.

Reduces Stress and Anxiety: A positive outlook can help to reduce stress and anxiety. It allows you to approach challenges with a more optimistic and solution-oriented mindset.

Improves Relationships: A positive and upbeat tone fosters more enjoyable and rewarding interactions. It creates a sense of warmth and connection with others.

<u>Increases Creativity and Productivity</u>: When you approach situations with a positive attitude, you're more likely to be creative, innovative, and productive.

ᐿᐿᐿ

Tips for Cultivating a Positive Tone:

<u>Focus on the Good</u>: Make a conscious effort to focus on the positive aspects of any situation.

<u>Use Positive Language</u>: Use words like "excited," "happy," "grateful," and "optimistic" in your conversations.

<u>Practice Active Listening</u>: When others share their experiences, listen attentively and offer words of encouragement and support.

<u>Find the Humor</u>: Look for the humor in everyday situations. A little laughter can go a long way in lifting your spirits and the spirits of those around you.

ᐿᐿᐿ

Fun Exercise: "The Gratitude Gratitude"

Start a gratitude journal and write down three things you're grateful for each day. This simple exercise can help shift your focus to the positive and cultivate a more optimistic outlook.

How does a positive attitude impact your interactions with others?

What are some of the ways you can cultivate a more positive outlook?

How can you use positive language to enhance your communication?

Maintaining a positive tone in your communication is not about being unrealistic or ignoring the challenges of life. It's about choosing to focus on the good, to see the best in others, and to approach life with a spirit of optimism and hope.

So, let your words be a beacon of positivity, and watch how it transforms your interactions and enriches your life.

Now go forth and spread some sunshine!

ᐿᐿᐿ

TWENTY-SIX

AVOID INTERRUPTING—IT ENSURES MUTUAL RESPECT

The Art of Listening: Why Interrupting is a Conversation Killer

Picture this: You're sharing a fascinating anecdote about your weekend adventure, brimming with excitement, when suddenly, "Hold on, hold on!" someone interrupts, eager to share their own story. It's like stepping on the brakes just as you're about to reach the most exciting part of a roller coaster! Frustrating, isn't it?

Interrupting others can derail conversations, stifle creativity, and even damage relationships. It's like trying to play a symphony with everyone playing at the same time – pure chaos!

The Power of Patient Listening:

Show Respect: When you allow others to finish their thoughts without interruption, you demonstrate respect for their ideas and their time. It shows that you value their perspective and are genuinely interested in what they have to say.

Foster Deeper Connections: Patient listening creates a safe and inviting space for open and honest communication. It allows others to feel heard and understood, which strengthens relationships.

Improve Understanding: By allowing others to fully express themselves, you gain a deeper understanding of their viewpoints and perspectives.

<u>Reduce Conflict:</u> Interrupting often leads to misunderstandings and arguments. By patiently listening, you create a more peaceful and harmonious communication environment.

ᏢᏢᏢ

Tips for Taming Your Inner Interrupter:

<u>Practice Active Listening:</u> Truly focus on what the other person is saying. Put away distractions, make eye contact, and use verbal cues like "I see," "Go on," and "That's interesting" to show that you're engaged.

<u>The "Two-Ears-One-Mouth" Rule:</u> Remember this simple rule: we have two ears and one mouth. Use them in proportion! Listen twice as much as you speak.

<u>The "Pause Button" Technique:</u> When you feel the urge to interrupt, mentally press the "pause" button. Take a deep breath and allow the other person to finish their thought.

<u>Embrace the Silence:</u> Don't be afraid of silence. Sometimes, a brief pause in the conversation can actually enhance communication and allow for deeper reflection.

Fun Fact:*Did you know that some cultures place a high value on silence and consider it a form of communication?*

Reflection Time:

When are you most likely to interrupt others?

What are the consequences of frequent interruptions?

How can you cultivate more patience in your communication?

Interrupting others can be a communication killer. By practicing patience and active listening, we can create a more respectful, understanding, and enjoyable communication experience for ourselves and those around us.

So, the next time you're in conversation, remember to let others finish their thoughts. You might be surprised at what you learn.

Now, go forth and conquer the art of patient listening! I promise you won't regret it.

ᏢᏢᏢ

TWENTY-SEVEN

RECOGNIZE ACHIEVEMENTS PUBLICLY—IT REINFORCES CONNECTIONS

Shining the Spotlight: The Power of Public Recognition

Imagine this: You've been working tirelessly on a project, pouring your heart and soul into it. And then, during a team meeting, your boss publicly acknowledges your hard work and dedication. How does that make you feel? Probably pretty darn good, right?

Public recognition is more than just a pat on the back. It's a powerful tool that can boost morale, motivate individuals, and strengthen team bonds.

The Magic of Public Appreciation:

<u>Boosting Morale</u>: When someone's achievements are recognized publicly, it gives them a sense of accomplishment and boosts their self-esteem. It makes them feel valued and appreciated.

<u>Motivating Others</u>: Public recognition motivates others to strive for excellence. It sets a positive example and encourages others to go above and beyond.

<u>Building Team Spirit</u>: When individuals are recognized for their contributions, it fosters a sense of camaraderie and team spirit. It reinforces

the idea that everyone's contributions are valued and appreciated.

<u>Creating a Positive Work Environment</u>: A culture of public recognition creates a more positive and motivating work environment. It encourages collaboration, teamwork, and a sense of shared success.

ᐧᐧᐧ

Tips for Effective Public Recognition:

<u>Be Specific and Sincere</u>: Instead of generic praise, be specific about the individual's contributions and what made them stand out.

<u>Make it Personal</u>: Tailor your recognition to the individual and their personality.

<u>Choose the Right Platform</u>: Public recognition can take many forms, from a simple "thank you" in a team meeting to a formal award ceremony.

<u>Lead by Example</u>: Managers and team leaders should model the behavior they wish to see by publicly recognizing the achievements of their team members.

Fun Fact: *Studies have shown that public recognition can have a significant impact on employee engagement, productivity, and job satisfaction.*

When was the last time you publicly recognized someone for their achievements?

How does it feel to be publicly recognized for your work?

How can you create a more culture of recognition in your workplace or within your social circles?

Public recognition is a simple yet powerful tool for building stronger relationships, boosting morale, and creating a more positive and motivating environment. So, the next time you witness someone going above and beyond, don't hesitate to publicly acknowledge their efforts.

You might be surprised at the positive impact it can have.

Let's celebrate each other's successes and create a world where everyone feels valued and appreciated!

ᐧᐧᐧ

TWENTY-EIGHT

BE APPROACHABLE—IT INVITES OPENNESS

The Open Door Policy: How Approachability Builds Stronger Connections

Let's face it, sometimes people can come across as intimidating, like a fortress with a "Keep Out" sign flashing above their heads. But what if you could radiate an aura of warmth and welcome, making others feel comfortable approaching you?

Being approachable is more than just having a friendly smile. It's about creating an atmosphere where others feel comfortable sharing their thoughts, ideas, and concerns. It's about building bridges of connection and fostering a sense of openness and trust.

The Magic of Approachability:

Fostering Open Communication: When you're approachable, people feel comfortable sharing their ideas, concerns, and feedback with you. This open communication leads to better decision-making, stronger teamwork, and increased creativity.

Building Stronger Relationships: Approachability fosters stronger relationships. People are more likely to connect with you on a deeper level when they feel comfortable and accepted.

Creating a Positive Atmosphere: An approachable demeanor creates a positive and welcoming environment for everyone. It encourages collaboration, teamwork, and a sense of community.

Boosting Confidence: When people feel comfortable approaching you, they feel more confident in themselves and their abilities.

ৡৡৡ

"

Tips for Becoming More Approachable:

Smile! A genuine smile can go a long way in making you appear more approachable and welcoming.

Make Eye Contact: Make consistent eye contact with others to show that you're engaged and interested in the conversation.

Use Open Body Language: Uncross your arms, lean forward slightly, and maintain an open and inviting posture.

Be an Active Listener: Truly listen to what others have to say, show empathy, and ask clarifying questions.

Initiate Conversation: Don't wait for others to approach you. Take the initiative to strike up conversations and connect with others.

Fun Fact: *Studies have shown that people who are perceived as approachable are often more successful in their careers and personal lives.*

How approachable do you think you are?

What are some ways you can improve your approachability?

How does approachability impact your relationships with others?

Being approachable is not just a social skill; it's a valuable life skill. By cultivating an approachable demeanor, you can build stronger relationships, foster a more positive and inclusive environment, and create a lasting positive impact on the world around you. So, open your doors, let your smile shine, and watch the connections blossom!

ᕲᕲᕲ

TWENTY-NINE
KEEP PROMISES—IT ESTABLISHES CREDIBILITY

A Promise Made, a Promise Kept: Building Trust Through Reliability

We've all been there. You make a promise, maybe to call a friend, finish a project by a certain date, or pick up groceries on your way home. And then...life happens. Things get hectic, distractions arise, and suddenly, that promise slips your mind.

But here's the thing: keeping your promises isn't just about avoiding disappointment. It's about building trust, demonstrating integrity, and showing others that you value your word.

The Power of Keeping Your Promises:

Building Trust: When you consistently keep your promises, you build trust and credibility with others. People know that they can rely on you, which strengthens your relationships.

Fostering Respect: Keeping your word demonstrates respect for others and their time. It shows that you value their needs and that you take your commitments seriously.

Increasing Self-Confidence: Keeping your promises boosts your self-esteem and confidence. It reinforces your sense of responsibility and personal integrity.

Creating a Positive Reputation: A reputation for reliability opens doors to new opportunities. People are more likely to trust you, work with you, and support you when they know you can be counted on.

ppp

Tips for Keeping Your Promises:

<u>Think Before You Speak</u>: Before making a promise, carefully consider whether you can realistically fulfill it.

<u>Set Realistic Expectations</u>: Don't overpromise and underdeliver.

<u>Use Reminders</u>: Set reminders on your phone or calendar to help you stay on track.

<u>Communicate Proactively</u>: If you anticipate that you won't be able to keep a promise, communicate with the other person as soon as possible and explain the situation.

ppp

Fun Fact:

The ancient Greeks believed that promises were sacred and that breaking a promise was a serious offense. They even had a god, Nemesis, who punished those who broke their oaths.

What are some promises you've made recently?

How important is keeping promises to you?

How does keeping promises impact your relationships with others?

Keeping your promises is a cornerstone of integrity and a foundation for strong relationships. It may seem like a small thing, but the impact of keeping your word can be significant. So, the next time you make a promise, remember the importance of keeping your word and the positive impact it can have on your life and the lives of those around you.

Now go forth and make and keep your promises with confidence!

ppp

THIRTY

SHARE UPLIFTING MESSAGES OR RESOURCES—IT BUILDS TRUST

Spreading Sunshine: The Power of Uplifting Messages

You know that feeling when you receive an unexpected compliment or a message of encouragement? It's like a little burst of sunshine on a cloudy day, instantly lifting your spirits. Sharing uplifting messages is more than just being nice; it's about creating a ripple effect of positivity that can brighten the lives of those around you.

The Magic of Uplifting Words:

<u>Boosting Morale:</u> A simple "You've got this!" or "I'm so proud of you!" can do wonders for someone's confidence and motivation.

<u>Creating a Positive Atmosphere:</u> Sharing uplifting messages creates a more positive and supportive environment. It fosters a sense of community and encourages others to thrive.

<u>Building Stronger Relationships:</u> Sharing words of encouragement strengthens bonds and deepens connections. It shows that you care about the other person and that you're invested in their success.

<u>Inspiring Others:</u> Uplifting messages can inspire others to reach their full potential and pursue their dreams.

❧❧❧

Spreading Positivity: A Daily Dose of Sunshine

The "Daily Dose of Inspiration" Habit: Start your day by reading an inspiring quote or listening to an uplifting podcast.

Leave Encouraging Notes: Leave little notes of encouragement for your loved ones, colleagues, or even strangers.

Share Positive News and Stories: Instead of dwelling on negativity, share uplifting news stories and inspiring stories of human kindness.

Offer Words of Support: When someone is facing a challenge, offer words of encouragement and support. Let them know you believe in them.

Fun Fact:

Studies have shown that expressing gratitude and sharing positive messages can actually increase your own happiness and well-being. It's a win-win situation!

When was the last time someone shared an uplifting message with you? How did it make you feel?

What are some ways you can spread more positivity in your daily life?

How can sharing uplifting messages make a difference in the world?

Sharing uplifting messages is a simple yet powerful way to make a positive impact on the world. It's like spreading sunshine – a little goes a long way. So, let your words be a beacon of hope, encouragement, and positivity. You never know how much your words might mean to someone else.

Now go forth and spread some sunshine!

ᴘᴘᴘ

THIRTY-ONE

USE HUMOR TO DIFFUSE TENSION—IT MAKES CONNECTIONS SMOOTHER

Laughter is the Best Medicine (for Communication Too!)

Let's face it, life can get a little tense sometimes. Whether it's a heated debate with a friend or a stressful situation at work, tension can quickly build and put a damper on any interaction. But what if I told you there's a secret weapon for diffusing tension and smoothing those communication bumps?

Humor: The Communication Lubricant

Humor is like a secret ingredient – it can transform any interaction from awkward to enjoyable.

<u>Breaking the Ice</u>: A well-timed joke or a playful tease can instantly break the ice and create a more relaxed and comfortable atmosphere.

<u>Diffusing Tension</u>: When things start to get heated, a touch of humor can defuse the situation. A lighthearted joke can help to ease tensions and shift the focus back to a more positive and productive conversation.

<u>Building Rapport</u>: Shared laughter creates a sense of connection and camaraderie. It fosters a feeling of warmth and camaraderie, making people feel more comfortable and open to communication.

<u>Making Difficult Conversations Easier</u>: Let's be honest, some conversations are just plain awkward. Humor can make these conversations

more bearable and even enjoyable.

ᚦᚦᚦ

Tips for Injecting Humor into Your Communication:

<u>Find the Funny</u>: Look for humor in everyday situations.

<u>Share a relevant anecdote</u>: A funny story can lighten the mood and illustrate your point in a memorable way.

<u>Use self-deprecating humor (with caution)</u>: A little self-deprecating humor can be disarming and endearing, but use it sparingly and with sensitivity.

<u>Read the room</u>: Not every situation calls for humor. Be mindful of the context and the other person's mood.

Fun Fact:

Laughter releases endorphins, natural mood boosters that have stress-reducing effects. So, by incorporating humor into your communication, you're not only improving your relationships, but you're also boosting your own well-being!

When was the last time you used humor to diffuse a tense situation?

How comfortable are you with using humor in your communication?

What are some ways you can incorporate more humor into your daily interactions?

Humor is a powerful tool for building stronger relationships, diffusing tension, and making communication more enjoyable. So, don't be afraid to inject a little laughter into your conversations. You might be surprised at how much it can improve your interactions and brighten your day.

Now go forth and spread some laughter! The world needs more of it.

ᚦᚦᚦ

THIRTY-TWO

RESPECT BOUNDARIES—IT ENSURES COMFORT IN RELATIONSHIPS

Respecting Boundaries: Building Bridges, Not Walls

Imagine this: You're having a lovely conversation with a friend when suddenly, they start giving unsolicited advice about your career, even though you never asked for it. It can feel a bit like someone barging into your personal space, right?

That's where the magic of respecting boundaries comes in. Boundaries are like invisible fences – they define where you end and the rest of the world begins. They help us protect our emotional, physical, and mental well-being.

The Power of Boundary Respect:

<u>Healthy Relationships</u>: Respecting boundaries is crucial for building and maintaining healthy relationships. It shows that you value the other person's feelings, needs, and autonomy.

<u>Reduced Stress and Anxiety</u>: When your boundaries are respected, you feel more in control and less stressed.

<u>Increased Self-Esteem</u>: Setting and enforcing healthy boundaries boosts your self-esteem. It shows that you value yourself and your needs.

<u>Improved Communication</u>: Clear boundaries encourage open and honest communication. They allow you to express your needs and expectations

clearly and respectfully.

᚛᚛᚛

Tips for Setting and Respecting Boundaries:

Identify Your Boundaries: What are your personal limits? What are you comfortable with and what are you not comfortable with?

Communicate Your Boundaries Clearly: Assertively and respectfully communicate your boundaries to others. For example, "I appreciate your concern, but I'd prefer to make my own decisions about this."

Respect Others' Boundaries: Just as you want your boundaries respected, be mindful of the boundaries of others.

Practice Self-Care: Setting boundaries is a form of self-care. It allows you to prioritize your own needs and well-being.

Fun Fact:

Did you know that even animals have a sense of personal space? They often use subtle cues, like tail wags or ear positions, to communicate their boundaries to other animals.

Reflection Questions:

What are some of your personal boundaries?

How can you communicate your boundaries more effectively?

How can you be more mindful of respecting the boundaries of others?

Respecting boundaries is not about being selfish or uncaring. It's about self-respect, self-care, and creating healthy and respectful relationships. So, let's all make a conscious effort to understand and respect the boundaries of those around us, and remember to firmly but kindly uphold our own.

Now go forth and build bridges of understanding, one boundary at a time!

᚛᚛᚛

THIRTY-THREE

USE TECHNOLOGY WISELY TO STAY IN TOUCH—IT BRIDGES GAPS

Bridging the Miles: The Magic of Technology in Connection

Remember those old-fashioned letters, the ones that took weeks to arrive? Snail mail, we called it. Seems like ages ago, doesn't it? Today, we have instant messaging, video calls, and social media connecting us with loved ones across the globe in the blink of an eye. Technology, for all its quirks, has truly revolutionized how we stay in touch.

The Tech-Tastic Power of Connection:

Bridging Distances: Technology has shrunk the world. We can connect with friends and family across continents with just a few taps on our phones. Video calls make it feel like we're sitting in the same room, even if we're miles apart.

Staying Connected During Life's Transitions: Whether you're moving to a new city, starting a new job, or going off to college, technology helps you stay connected to your support network.

Sharing Experiences: From photos and videos to live streams, technology allows us to share our experiences and adventures with loved ones in real-time.

Building Communities: Social media platforms and online communities bring together people with shared interests, fostering a sense of belonging and connection.

ᐅᐅᐅ

Tips for Tech-Savvy Socializing:

<u>Quality over Quantity</u>: Prioritize meaningful interactions over superficial ones. Instead of scrolling endlessly, schedule dedicated time for video calls with loved ones.

<u>Mindful Tech Use</u>: Be mindful of your screen time and ensure that technology doesn't interfere with your real-life relationships.

<u>Use Tech to Enhance, Not Replace</u>: Technology should complement your in-person interactions, not replace them.

<u>Be Present</u>: When you're with friends and family, put your phone down and be present in the moment.

Fun Fact: Did you know that the first text message was sent in 1992? It simply read, "Merry Christmas."

Reflection Questions:

How has technology changed the way you connect with loved ones?

What are some of your favorite ways to use technology to stay in touch?

How can you use technology more mindfully to enhance your relationships?

Technology, when used wisely, can be a powerful tool for connecting with others and building stronger relationships. So, embrace the power of technology, but remember to use it mindfully to enrich your life and foster meaningful connections with the people you care about.

Now go forth and connect! The world is waiting.

ᐅᐅᐅ

THIRTY-FOUR

ENCOURAGE OTHERS TO SHARE THEIR STORIES—IT BUILDS TRUST

The Storytelling Circle: Encouraging Others to Share

Have you ever noticed how captivating it is to listen to someone share a personal story? Whether it's a funny childhood memory, an overcoming-the-odds tale, or a poignant reflection on life, stories have a unique power to connect us on a deeper level.

Encouraging others to share their stories isn't just about being polite; it's about creating a safe and supportive space where people feel valued and heard.

The Magic of Encouraging Storytelling:

<u>Building Trust and Intimacy</u>: When you encourage someone to share their story, you're essentially saying, "I'm interested in you and your experiences." This builds trust and fosters deeper connections.

<u>Fostering Empathy and Understanding</u>: Sharing stories helps us see the world through another person's eyes. It cultivates empathy and allows us to understand and appreciate different perspectives.

<u>Creating a Sense of Community</u>: When people share their stories, they feel a sense of belonging and connection. It fosters a sense of community where everyone feels valued and heard.

<u>Unlocking Hidden Gems</u>: You never know what gems you might uncover when you encourage others to share their stories. You might hear inspiring tales of resilience, learn valuable life lessons, or discover hidden talents.

ᐅᐅᐅ

Tips for Encouraging Storytelling:

<u>Ask Open-Ended Questions</u>: Instead of asking "How was your day?", try asking "What was the highlight of your day?" or "What made you smile today?"

<u>Be an Active Listener</u>: When someone starts sharing a story, give them your full attention. Make eye contact, nod your head, and use encouraging verbal cues like "Wow," "That's interesting," and "Tell me more."

<u>Create a Safe and Supportive Space</u>: Let people know that they can share their stories without judgment.

Share Your Own Stories: By sharing your own stories, you create a safe and inviting space for others to do the same.

Fun Fact: Storytelling is one of the oldest forms of human communication. It's how we passed down history, shared cultural values, and entertained ourselves for generations.

Reflection Questions:

When was the last time you encouraged someone to share their story?

How does it feel to share your own stories with others?

How can you create a more storytelling-friendly environment in your daily interactions?

Encouraging others to share their stories is a simple yet powerful way to build stronger connections, foster empathy, and create a more meaningful and compassionate world. So, the next time you're in conversation, remember to create a space where people feel comfortable sharing their unique stories. You might be surprised at the profound impact it can have.

Now go forth and listen with an open heart and an eager mind. You never know what amazing stories you might uncover!

ᐅᐅᐅ

THIRTY-FIVE

END CONVERSATIONS ON A POSITIVE NOTE—IT LEAVES A LASTING IMPRESSION

The "Goodbye" Glow: Ending Conversations on a High Note

Think about your favorite movies. Don't they usually end with a satisfying resolution? A happy ending, a heartwarming moment, a sense of closure? Conversations work the same way! How you end a conversation can significantly impact your overall impression and leave a lasting impression.

The Power of a Positive Goodbye:

<u>Leaving a Lasting Good Impression</u>: Ending a conversation on a positive note leaves a lasting positive impression. It leaves the other person with a good feeling and makes them more likely to want to connect with you again.

<u>Building Stronger Relationships</u>: Positive endings foster a sense of warmth and connection. They create a sense of goodwill and leave both parties feeling valued and appreciated.

<u>Setting a Positive Tone</u>: Ending on a positive note sets a positive tone for future interactions. It creates a sense of optimism and encourages further communication.

<u>Reducing Awkwardness</u>: A positive ending can help to avoid awkward silences or abrupt departures, making the overall interaction more enjoyable.

❦❦❦

Tips for Ending Conversations on a High Note:

<u>Express Gratitude</u>: Thank the other person for their time and for the conversation. For example, "Thank you for taking the time to chat with me."

<u>Summarize Key Takeaways</u>: Briefly summarize the key takeaways from the conversation. This reinforces the key points and shows that you were actively listening.

<u>Offer a Positive Outlook</u>: End the conversation on an optimistic note. For example, "I'm looking forward to our next conversation." or "I hope you have a wonderful rest of your day."

<u>Use a Warm and Friendly Tone</u>: Maintain a friendly and upbeat tone throughout the conversation, especially during the closing.

Fun Fact: Did you know that in many cultures, specific greetings and farewells are used to show respect and politeness?

Reflection Questions:

How do you typically end your conversations?

What impact do you think your current conversation-ending style has on your relationships?

How can you incorporate more positive endings into your interactions?

Ending conversations on a positive note is a simple yet powerful way to enhance your communication skills and build stronger relationships. It's like adding a sprinkle of magic dust to the end of your interactions. So, next time you're wrapping up a conversation, remember to leave a lasting good impression with a positive and uplifting closing.

Now go forth and spread positivity with every conversation!

ᗡᗡᗡ

"Ways to Influence" Focus on persuasion, storytelling, and negotiation

THIRTY-SIX

START WITH A POWERFUL OPENING LINE- IT GRABS ATTENTION

Hook, Line, and Sinker: The Power of a Captivating Opening

Imagine you're reading a book. The first sentence is crucial, isn't it? It's the hook that pulls you in, making you want to turn the page and discover what happens next. The same principle applies to any form of communication – from a casual conversation to a persuasive presentation.

A strong opening line is like a magician's first trick – it grabs attention, piques curiosity, and sets the stage for what's to come.

The Art of the Captivating Opening:

Persuasion:

Start with a startling statistic: "Did you know that..."

Pose a thought-provoking question: "What if I told you..."

Appeal to emotions: "Imagine a world where..."

Storytelling:

Begin with a captivating anecdote: "It all started on a rainy Tuesday afternoon..."

Use vivid imagery: "The air was thick with the scent of rain..."

Create suspense: "I never expected what happened next..."

Negotiation:

Acknowledge the other person's perspective: "I understand your concerns about..."

Focus on shared goals: "Let's work together to find a solution that benefits us both."

Offer a win-win solution: "I propose a compromise that..."

 קקק

Fun Fact:

The first line of Jane Austen's "Pride and Prejudice" is considered one of the most famous opening lines in literature: "It is a truth universally acknowledged, that a single man in possession of a good fortune, must be in want of a wife."

Reflection Questions:

What are some of your favorite opening lines from books, movies, or songs?

How can you use strong opening lines to improve your own communication?

Experiment with different opening lines in your next conversation. What impact do they have?

Mastering the art of the opening line can significantly enhance your communication skills. Whether you're trying to persuade someone, tell a captivating story, or simply make a strong first impression, a well-crafted opening line can set the stage for success.

So, the next time you're about to communicate, take a moment to craft a compelling opening. You might be surprised at how much it can impact the outcome.

Now go forth and captivate your audience with your words!

קקק

THIRTY-SEVEN

USE "WE" INSTEAD OF "I" – TO FOSTER COLLABORATION

The Power of "We": Fostering Collaboration Through Shared Language

Ever noticed how using phrases like "we" and "our" in a conversation can subtly shift the dynamic? It's like a magic wand that transforms a solo act into a collaborative performance.

****The "We" Effect:**

<u>Building Camaraderie</u>: Using "we" language instantly creates a sense of togetherness. It fosters a feeling of shared purpose and encourages collaboration. Instead of emphasizing individual achievements, it highlights collective success.

<u>Promoting Teamwork</u>: In a team setting, "we" language fosters a sense of shared responsibility and accountability. It encourages team members to work together towards a common goal.

<u>Enhancing Persuasion</u>: In persuasive situations, using "we" language can be incredibly powerful. It creates a sense of shared interest and encourages the other party to see the situation from your perspective. For example, instead of saying "I think we should do it this way," try "Let's work together to achieve this goal."

<u>Negotiation Superpower</u>: During negotiations, using "we" language can help to break down barriers and find mutually beneficial solutions. It shifts the focus from individual gain to a collective outcome.

"We" Language in Action:

Instead of: "I believe this is the best approach."
Try: "Let's explore this approach together."
Instead of: "My proposal is the most effective."
Try: "I believe this proposal offers the best outcome for our team."
Instead of: "You need to do this..."
Try: "Let's work together to ensure this is completed successfully."

Fun Fact:

Research has shown that using inclusive language, such as "we" and "our," can increase trust and cooperation among team members.

Reflection Questions:

How often do you use "we" language in your daily conversations?

What are some situations where using "we" language would be particularly effective?

How can you incorporate more "we" language into your communication to foster a more collaborative and inclusive environment?

Using "we" language is a simple yet powerful technique for fostering collaboration, building stronger relationships, and achieving shared goals. So, the next time you're in a conversation, remember the power of "we" and let it guide your communication.

Now go forth and build stronger connections through the magic of shared language!

ᗡᗡᗡ

THIRTY-EIGHT

SHARE STORIES THAT RESONATE EMOTIONALLY- FACTS TELL, STORIES SELL

The Storytelling Spark: Igniting Hearts and Minds

Okay, let's ditch the boring facts and figures for a moment. Imagine you're trying to convince your friend to try a new restaurant. You could say, "They have the best sushi in town, according to Yelp."

Or, you could say, "I took my parents there last week, and my dad, who's a notoriously picky eater, declared it the best sushi he's ever had. He even ordered extra ginger!"

See the difference? Stories have a magical way of connecting with people on an emotional level. They paint pictures in our minds, evoke feelings, and make us feel like we're part of the experience.

The Power of Emotionally Resonant Stories:

<u>Persuasion Supercharged</u>: Facts tell, stories sell. When you use stories to illustrate your point, you tap into people's emotions and make your message more persuasive.

<u>Building Deeper Connections</u>: Sharing stories creates a sense of shared experience. It allows others to connect with you on a deeper level and understand your perspective.

<u>Making Information Memorable</u>: Stories are far more memorable than dry facts and figures. They stick in your mind long after the conversation is

over.

Inspiring Action: Stories can inspire and motivate others. They can show people what's possible and encourage them to take action.

ᗕᗕᗕ

Tips for Weaving Emotion into Your Storytelling:

Find the Emotional Core: What's the underlying emotion of your story? Is it joy, sadness, fear, or hope?

Use Vivid Language: Paint a picture with your words. Use vivid imagery, sensory details, and emotional language to bring your story to life.

Connect with Your Audience: Tailor your stories to your audience. What kind of stories will resonate with them?

Practice, Practice, Practice: The more you tell stories, the better you'll become at crafting narratives that are both engaging and emotionally resonant.

Fun Fact:

Research has shown that stories activate multiple areas of the brain, including those associated with emotion, empathy, and decision-making.

Reflection Questions:

What are some stories that have had a significant impact on you?

How can you incorporate more storytelling into your daily communication?

How can you use storytelling to more effectively persuade, inspire, and connect with others?

Stories are the lifeblood of human connection. They entertain us, inspire us, and teach us valuable lessons about life. By mastering the art of storytelling and weaving emotion into your narratives, you can become a more persuasive, engaging, and impactful communicator.

So, go forth and share your stories with the world! Let your words paint pictures, evoke emotions, and inspire action.

ᗕᗕᗕ

THIRTY-NINE

FRAME YOUR IDEAS WITH BENEFITS FOR THE LISTENER

The "What's In It For Them?" Factor: Framing Your Ideas for Impact

Ever tried to convince someone of something, only to have them glaze over? It can feel like talking to a brick wall, right?

The key to effective communication isn't just about what you say, but how you say it. Framing your ideas with the listener's benefits in mind is like adding a sprinkle of magic – it makes your message more compelling, persuasive, and likely to be received with open arms.

The "WIIFM" Factor (What's In It For Me?):

<u>Persuasion Powerhouse</u>: When you frame your ideas around the benefits the listener will receive, you tap into their self-interest. This makes your message more persuasive and increases the likelihood that they'll be receptive to your ideas.

<u>Building Rapport</u>: By focusing on the listener's needs and desires, you demonstrate empathy and understanding. This builds rapport and strengthens your relationship with the other person.

<u>Negotiation Advantage</u>: In a negotiation, framing your proposals in terms of mutual benefit increases the chances of reaching a mutually agreeable solution.

<u>Increased Engagement</u>: When people understand how your ideas can benefit them, they're more likely to be engaged and invested in the conversation.

ᗡᗡᗡ

Tips for Framing Your Ideas with "WIIFM":

<u>Ask Yourself</u>: "What's in it for them?" Before presenting your ideas, take a moment to consider the benefits that the listener will receive.

<u>Use "You" Statements</u>: Instead of focusing on "I" or "me," use "you" statements to highlight the benefits for the listener. For example, "You'll be able to..." or "This will help you to..."

<u>Tell a Story</u>: Frame your ideas within a compelling story that illustrates the benefits to the listener.

<u>Focus on Solutions, Not Problems</u>: Instead of dwelling on the problems, focus on the solutions and how they will benefit the listener.

Fun Fact:

Great salespeople understand the power of "WIIFM." They focus on how their products or services will benefit the customer, rather than simply listing features and specifications.

How can you incorporate "WIIFM" into your everyday conversations?

How can framing your ideas with the listener's benefits in mind improve your persuasive skills?

Think of a recent situation where you could have better framed your ideas with "WIIFM" in mind. How could you have approached it differently?

Framing your ideas with the listener's benefits in mind is a powerful communication strategy. By focusing on "WIIFM," you can increase your persuasiveness, build stronger relationships, and achieve greater success in all your interactions. So, the next time you're trying to convince someone of something, remember to put yourself in their shoes and consider what's in it for them. You might be surprised at how much more receptive they are to your ideas!

ᗡᗡᗡ

FORTY

ASK OPEN-ENDED QUESTIONS TO GUIDE THE CONVERSATION

The Art of the Open-Ended Question: Unlocking Deeper Conversations

Imagine this: You're at a party, and you ask someone, "Do you like this music?" They reply with a simple "Yes." Conversation over.

Now, imagine asking, "What are your thoughts on the music playing?" Suddenly, the door to deeper conversation swings wide open.

Open-ended questions are the secret weapon of engaging communicators. They go beyond simple yes-or-no answers, encouraging deeper reflection, richer dialogue, and a more nuanced understanding.

The Power of Open-Ended Questions:

Unleashing the Flow of Information: Open-ended questions invite the other person to share their thoughts, feelings, and experiences in their own words. This provides valuable insights that you wouldn't get with simple yes-or-no questions.

Building Deeper Connections: When you ask open-ended questions, you show genuine interest in the other person's perspective. This fosters a sense of connection and builds stronger relationships.

Fostering Creativity and Critical Thinking: Open-ended questions encourage the other person to think critically, analyze information, and express their own unique ideas.

Improving Persuasion and Negotiation: By asking open-ended questions, you can better understand the other person's needs and concerns, which can help you to tailor your message and reach a mutually beneficial agreement.

ᐅᐅᐅ

Mastering the Art of the Open-Ended Question:

Start with "Who," "What," "Why," "How," "Tell me more about..." These words are the gateway to deeper conversations.

<u>Listen Actively</u>: Pay close attention to their response and use follow-up questions to delve deeper.

<u>Be Patient and Allow for Pause</u>: Give the other person time to think and formulate their response.

<u>Practice, Practice, Practice</u>: The more you use open-ended questions, the more natural they will become.

Fun Fact:

Socratic questioning, a method of philosophical inquiry, relies heavily on open-ended questions to encourage critical thinking and deeper understanding.

Reflection Questions:

How often do you use open-ended questions in your conversations?

What are some examples of open-ended questions you could use in your next conversation?

How can you use open-ended questions to improve your communication skills in various settings (e.g., work, social, family)?

Open-ended questions are the keys to unlocking deeper conversations, building stronger relationships, and gaining a richer understanding of the world around you. So, the next time you're in conversation, ditch the yes-or-no questions and embrace the power of open-ended inquiries. You might be surprised at the fascinating conversations that unfold.

Now go forth and explore the depths of human connection through the power of open-ended questions!

ᐅᐅᐅ

FORTY-ONE

USE THE POWER OF PAUSES- SILENCE CAN BE PERSUASIVE

Silence Speaks Volumes

We live in a world that hates silence. Phones buzz, notifications chime, and the constant chatter of the outside world fills every gap. But what if I told you that silence, that often-feared void, is actually a powerful communication tool?

Believe it or not, silence can be more persuasive than words. It's a subtle art, a moment of stillness that allows for reflection, creates impact, and strengthens connection.

The Art of the Strategic Pause:

****Persuasion:**

<u>Building Suspense</u>: In a negotiation, a strategic pause after making a bold statement can increase its impact. It gives the other party time to consider your proposal and creates a sense of anticipation.

<u>Highlighting Importance</u>: Pausing before delivering crucial information emphasizes its significance. It creates a sense of drama and makes your message more memorable.

Storytelling:

<u>Creating Dramatic Effect</u>: A well-placed pause can heighten the tension and suspense in a story. It allows the listener to imagine the scene and anticipate what happens next.

<u>Emphasizing Key Moments</u>: Pausing before revealing a crucial plot point adds dramatic weight and makes the story more impactful.

Negotiation:

<u>Creating Space for Reflection</u>: A pause during a negotiation allows both parties to reflect on their positions and consider alternative solutions.

<u>Demonstrating Confidence</u>: A confident pause can convey a sense of assurance and strengthen your negotiating position.

Fun Fact:

Silence is a powerful communication tool in many cultures. In some Eastern philosophies, silence is considered a gateway to deeper understanding and inner peace.

Reflection Questions:

When was the last time you used silence effectively in a conversation?

How can you incorporate strategic pauses into your presentations, negotiations, and storytelling?

What does silence communicate to you when someone else uses it during a conversation?

Silence may seem like an absence of communication, but in reality, it's a powerful tool. By strategically using pauses in your conversations, you can enhance your communication, increase your influence, and create a more impactful and memorable experience for yourself and others.

So, the next time you're in a conversation, don't be afraid to embrace the power of silence. You might be surprised at the impact it can have.

Now go forth and master the art of the strategic pause!

ᑭᑭᑭ

FORTY-TWO

SIMPLIFY YOUR MESSAGE- CLARITY BUILDS INFLUENCE

Cutting Through the Noise: The Power of Clarity

Imagine trying to assemble IKEA furniture without instructions. Chaos, right? Communication is a lot like that. If your message is cluttered with jargon, jargon, and more jargon, it's like trying to assemble that furniture blindfolded.

Clarity is the key. It's about stripping away the fluff and getting straight to the point. When your message is clear, it's not only easier to understand, but it's also more persuasive, more impactful, and more likely to achieve its intended goal.

The Magic of Clarity:

Persuasion Powerhouse: Clear communication is the foundation of effective persuasion. When your message is concise and easy to understand, your audience is more likely to be convinced by your arguments.

Building Trust and Credibility: Clear and concise communication builds trust and credibility. It shows that you respect your audience's time and that you value clear and effective communication.

Improved Decision-Making: When information is presented clearly and concisely, it's easier to understand, analyze, and make informed decisions.

Increased Efficiency: Clear communication reduces misunderstandings and confusion, which saves time and improves efficiency.

ᛩᛩᛩ

Tips for Communicating with Clarity:

<u>Know Your Audience</u>: Tailor your message to your audience. Avoid using jargon or technical terms that they may not understand.

<u>Focus on Key Messages</u>: Identify the most important points you want to convey and stick to them.

<u>Use Simple Language</u>: Avoid using complex words and convoluted sentences.

<u>Practice Active Listening</u>: Pay attention to how your message is being received. Are there any signs of confusion?

Fun Fact:

Abraham Lincoln was renowned for his ability to communicate complex ideas in a clear and concise manner. His Gettysburg Address, one of the most famous speeches in American history, is a masterclass in concise and impactful communication.

Reflection Questions:

How clear and concise is your own communication style?

What are some areas where you could improve the clarity of your communication?

How can you use clear communication to improve your relationships, your career, and your overall success?

Clarity is the cornerstone of effective communication. By simplifying your message and focusing on the key takeaways, you can increase your impact, build stronger relationships, and achieve your goals more effectively. So, the next time you communicate, remember to cut through the noise and deliver your message with clarity and impact.

Now go forth and conquer the world with your crystal-clear communication!

ନନନ

FORTY-THREE

PROVIDE EVIDENCE TO BACK YOUR CLAIMS- CREDIBILITY MATTERS

Backed by Facts: The Power of Evidence in Communication

Imagine trying to convince someone that the Earth is round. You could just say, "Trust me, it's true!" But wouldn't it be more convincing to present evidence like photos from space, scientific explanations, and historical accounts of exploration?

Just like astronauts need evidence to prove their theories, we need evidence to support our claims in everyday communication.

The Power of Evidence:

<u>Boosting Credibility</u>: When you back up your claims with evidence, you build trust and credibility. People are more likely to believe you when you can support your statements with facts, data, or examples.

<u>Increasing Persuasion</u>: Evidence makes your arguments more persuasive. It strengthens your position and makes it harder for others to dispute your claims.

<u>Improving Decision-Making</u>: Evidence helps people make informed decisions. When you present information backed by evidence, you empower others to make the best possible choices.

<u>Fostering Critical Thinking</u>: When you present evidence, you encourage others to think critically and evaluate information for themselves.

ᑭᑭᑭ

Tips for Using Evidence Effectively:

<u>Gather Reliable Evidence</u>: Use credible sources like research studies, expert opinions, and reputable news outlets.

<u>Present Evidence Clearly and Concisely</u>: Avoid overwhelming your audience with too much information. Present your evidence in a clear, concise, and easy-to-understand manner.

<u>Use Examples and Stories</u>: Illustrate your points with relevant examples and stories. This makes your message more engaging and memorable.

<u>Acknowledge Counterarguments</u>: Be prepared to address potential counterarguments and provide evidence to refute them.

Fun Fact:

The scientific method is built on the foundation of evidence. Scientists use observation, experimentation, and data analysis to gather evidence and test their hypotheses.

Reflection Questions:

How often do you use evidence to support your claims in your daily conversations?

What are some examples of situations where you could use evidence more effectively?

How can you improve your ability to gather and present evidence to support your arguments?

In today's world, information is readily available. But not all information is created equal. By backing up your claims with credible evidence, you can enhance your communication, build trust, and make a more significant impact on the world around you.

So, the next time you want to make a point, remember to arm yourself with the power of evidence. You'll be amazed at how much stronger your message becomes.

ᗐᗐᗐ

FORTY-FOUR

SHOW EMPATHY- IT BUILDS DEEPER CONNECTIONS

Walking in Someone Else's Shoes: The Power of Empathy in Communication

Imagine this: You're trying to convince your friend to try a new restaurant. Instead of just rattling off the menu, you say, "I know you love spicy food, and they have this incredible Sichuan peppercorn dish that I think you'd absolutely adore."

See the difference? That's empathy in action. It's about understanding and sharing the feelings of others, and it's a powerful tool in communication.

The Magic of Empathy:

<u>Building Stronger Connections</u>: When you show empathy, you create a deeper connection with the other person. They feel heard, understood, and valued, which strengthens your bond.

<u>Increasing Persuasion</u>: People are more likely to be persuaded by someone who understands their needs and concerns. Empathy helps you tailor your message to resonate with their emotions and values.

<u>Fostering Collaboration</u>: In a team setting, empathy fosters a more collaborative and supportive environment. It encourages team members to understand and respect each other's perspectives.

<u>Resolving Conflicts Peacefully</u>: When you approach conflicts with empathy, you're more likely to find common ground and reach a mutually

agreeable solution.

ᗞᗞᗞ

Tips for Cultivating Empathy in Your Communication:

<u>Active Listening</u>: Truly listen to what the other person is saying, both verbally and nonverbally. Pay attention to their tone of voice, body language, and emotions.

<u>Put Yourself in Their Shoes</u>: Try to see the situation from their perspective. Ask yourself, "How would I feel if I were in their situation?"

<u>Validate Their Feelings</u>: Acknowledge and validate the other person's emotions. For example, "I understand why you feel frustrated."

<u>Use Empathetic Language</u>: Use phrases like "I understand," "I can see why you feel that way," and "I appreciate your perspective."

ᗞᗞᗞ

The "Empathy Map" Exercise:

Choose a person or situation: Select a person or situation where you want to improve your empathy.

Gather Information: Gather as much information as possible about the person or situation.

Create an Empathy Map: Draw a simple diagram with four quadrants:

Thinking: What is this person thinking? What are their beliefs and assumptions?

Feeling: What emotions are they experiencing? How are they feeling about the situation?

Saying: What are they saying (both verbally and nonverbally)?

Doing: What are they doing or likely to do in this situation?

Step into Their Shoes: Based on the information you've gathered, try to step into their shoes and experience the situation from their perspective.

ᗞᗞᗞ

Reflection Questions:

When was the last time you demonstrated empathy in a conversation?

What are some situations where you could benefit from cultivating more empathy?

How can you use empathy to improve your communication and build stronger relationships?

Empathy is the cornerstone of effective communication. By understanding and sharing the feelings of others, we can build stronger connections, resolve conflicts more effectively, and create a more compassionate and understanding world. So, the next time you're in conversation, try to step into the other person's shoes and experience the world from their perspective. You might be surprised at how much it changes your interactions.

Now go forth and spread empathy like sunshine!

FORTY-FIVE

HIGHLIGHT THE "WHY" BEHIND YOUR MESSAGE- IT'S WHAT INSPIRES ACTION

Beyond the "What": Unlocking Influence with the "Why"

Imagine trying to convince your friend to go hiking with you. You could say, "We should go hiking this weekend." (That's a statement, not very inspiring.) Or, you could say, "Imagine waking up early, breathing in the fresh mountain air, and enjoying breathtaking views. It'll be an incredible way to clear our heads and reconnect with nature."

See the difference? The second statement focuses on the why – the benefits and the emotional experience. It's like adding a sprinkle of magic dust to your communication, making it more compelling and persuasive.

The Power of "Why":

Persuasion Supercharged: When you communicate the "why" behind your message, you tap into people's emotions and motivations. This makes your message more resonant and increases the likelihood of them taking action.

Building Deeper Connections: Sharing the "why" behind your ideas and actions fosters a deeper level of connection. It allows others to understand your motivations and see the bigger picture.

Inspiring Action: When people understand the "why" behind a cause or initiative, they are more likely to be inspired to take action and get involved.

Negotiation Advantage: In a negotiation, focusing on the "why" behind your proposals can help you build common ground and find mutually beneficial solutions.

ᗡᗡᗡ

Tips for Communicating Your "Why":

Tell a Story: Frame your message within a compelling story that illustrates the "why" behind your ideas.

Use Emotional Language: Appeal to the listener's emotions by using words that evoke feelings of excitement, joy, hope, or inspiration.

Focus on Shared Values: Connect your "why" to shared values and common goals.

Practice Active Listening: Pay attention to the listener's responses and adjust your message accordingly.

Fun Fact:

The renowned motivational speaker Simon Sinek popularized the concept of "Start with Why" in his TED Talk, emphasizing the importance of understanding the underlying purpose and values behind any endeavor.

Reflection Questions:

How often do you explicitly communicate the "why" behind your ideas and actions?

What are some situations where clearly communicating your "why" would be particularly beneficial?

How can you improve your ability to articulate your "why" in a compelling and persuasive manner?

The "why" is the heart and soul of any message. By clearly articulating your purpose and motivations, you can inspire action, build stronger connections, and achieve greater success in all your endeavors. So, the next time you communicate, remember to ask yourself, "Why?" and then share that "why" with the world.

Now go forth and inspire others with the power of your "why"!

ᗡᗡᗡ

FORTY-SIX

USE METAPHORS OR ANALOGIES—THEY MAKE COMPLEX IDEAS RELATABLE

Painting Pictures with Words: The Power of Metaphors and Analogies

Ever tried to explain a complex concept to someone, only to find yourself lost in a sea of jargon? It's like trying to describe the taste of chocolate to someone who's never had it. Frustrating, right?

That's where the magic of metaphors and analogies comes in. These literary devices are like secret weapons for communication, transforming abstract ideas into relatable and memorable images.

The Power of Figurative Language:

<u>Persuasion Supercharged</u>: Metaphors and analogies make your message more engaging and persuasive. They tap into our imaginations and emotions, making your ideas more memorable and impactful.

<u>Building Deeper Understanding</u>: By comparing unfamiliar concepts to familiar ones, you help your audience grasp complex ideas more easily. It's like a bridge connecting the unknown to the known.

<u>Fostering Creativity</u>: Using metaphors and analogies encourages creative thinking and helps you to explore ideas from different perspectives.

<u>Making Communication More Engaging</u>: Let's face it, metaphors and analogies make communication more interesting! They add a touch of color and personality to your words.

ϷϷϷ

Tips for Using Metaphors and Analogies Effectively:

Choose the Right Comparison: Select metaphors and analogies that are relevant, relatable, and easy to understand.

Use Vivid Imagery: Paint a picture with your words. Use sensory details to make your metaphors and analogies come alive.

Practice, Practice, Practice: Experiment with different metaphors and analogies to find what works best for you.

Be Mindful of Your Audience: Tailor your metaphors and analogies to your audience. What resonates with them?

Fun Fact:

Shakespeare was a master of metaphors and analogies. His plays are filled with vivid imagery and powerful metaphors that continue to resonate with audiences today.

Can you think of any metaphors or analogies that you use frequently in your everyday conversations?

How can you incorporate more metaphors and analogies into your communication to make it more engaging and impactful?

What are some common metaphors or analogies that you encounter in your daily life?

Metaphors and analogies are powerful tools that can transform your communication. By using these literary devices effectively, you can make your message more engaging, persuasive, and memorable. So, the next time you're struggling to explain a complex idea, try reaching for a metaphor. You might be surprised at how easily your message comes to life.

Now go forth and paint your words with vivid imagery!

ϷϷϷ

FORTY-SEVEN

FOCUS ON SHARED GOALS—IT ALIGNS INTERESTS

Finding Common Ground: The Power of Shared Goals

Imagine you're trying to convince your family to go on a camping trip. You could focus on how much you want to go, how relaxing it will be for you, and how much you've been looking forward to it.

But what if you instead focused on how much fun the whole family would have together? How it would be a chance to disconnect from technology, spend quality time together, and create lasting memories?

That's the power of focusing on shared goals. It shifts the focus from individual desires to collective aspirations, creating a sense of unity and encouraging collaboration.

The Magic of Shared Goals:

<u>Persuasion Supercharged</u>: When you frame your ideas around shared goals, you're more likely to persuade others to support you. People are naturally drawn to opportunities that benefit the group as a whole.

<u>Building Stronger Relationships</u>: Focusing on shared goals strengthens relationships by fostering a sense of shared purpose and collective responsibility.

<u>Promoting Collaboration</u>: When everyone is working towards a common goal, collaboration becomes easier and more natural.

<u>Resolving Conflicts Peacefully</u>: By identifying shared goals, you can find common ground and work together to find solutions that benefit everyone.

ԾԾԾ

Tips for Focusing on Shared Goals:

<u>Identify Common Ground</u>: Before presenting your ideas, take the time to identify shared interests, values, and goals.

<u>Use "We" Language</u>: Frame your proposals using "we" language. For example, instead of saying "I think we should do this," try "Let's work together to achieve this goal."

<u>Highlight the Benefits for Everyone</u>: Clearly articulate how your proposal will benefit everyone involved.

<u>Be Flexible and Willing to Compromise</u>: Be open to adjusting your ideas to ensure that they align with the shared goals of the group.

Fun Fact:

Many successful companies and organizations thrive because they have a clear and compelling shared vision that unites their employees and inspires them to work together towards a common goal.

Reflection Questions:

How often do you consider shared goals in your interactions with others?

What are some examples of situations where focusing on shared goals could be particularly beneficial?

How can you better identify and communicate shared goals in your own life?

Focusing on shared goals is a powerful strategy for building stronger relationships, fostering collaboration, and achieving collective success. By aligning your efforts with the common good, you can create a more positive and fulfilling experience for everyone involved.

So, the next time you're trying to persuade someone or work towards a common goal, remember to focus on the "we" and the "why." You might be surprised at how much more effective your communication becomes.

ԾԾԾ

FORTY-EIGHT

PRACTICE ACTIVE LISTENING—IT MAKES THE OTHER PERSON FEEL VALUED

The Art of True Listening: How Active Listening Builds Stronger Connections

Imagine you're telling a friend about a challenging situation you faced. You're pouring your heart out, and they're busy scrolling through their phone, occasionally muttering "uh-huh" without really paying attention. Doesn't exactly make you feel heard, does it?

Active listening is more than just hearing the words someone says. It's about truly engaging with the speaker, showing them that you value their thoughts and feelings.

The Magic of Active Listening:

<u>Building Stronger Relationships</u>: When you truly listen to someone, you build trust and strengthen your connection. They feel valued, understood, and respected.

<u>Fostering Empathy and Understanding</u>: Active listening helps you to see the world from the other person's perspective. It cultivates empathy and allows you to connect with them on a deeper level.

<u>Resolving Conflicts Peacefully</u>: When you truly listen to the other person's concerns, you're more likely to find common ground and resolve conflicts peacefully.

<u>Improving Persuasion and Negotiation</u>: By actively listening to the other person's needs and concerns, you can tailor your message and approach to be more persuasive and effective.

ᑭᑭᑭ

Tips for Becoming an Active Listener:

<u>Focus on the Speaker</u>: Give the speaker your full attention. Put away distractions, make eye contact, and avoid interrupting.

<u>Use Non-Verbal Cues</u>: Nod your head, use encouraging gestures, and maintain open and inviting body language.

<u>Reflect and Summarize</u>: Paraphrase what the speaker has said to ensure you understand their message correctly. For example, "So, if I understand correctly, you're saying..."

<u>Ask Clarifying Questions</u>: Ask open-ended questions to encourage the speaker to elaborate on their thoughts and feelings.

ᑭᑭᑭ

Fun Fact:

Research has shown that active listening can significantly improve job performance, enhance leadership skills, and increase employee satisfaction.

Reflection Questions:

How often do you find yourself truly listening to others?

What are some of your biggest distractions when trying to listen?

How can you improve your active listening skills in your daily interactions?

Active listening is a valuable life skill that can significantly improve your communication and relationships. By truly listening to others, you show them that you value their perspective, build stronger connections, and create a more understanding and compassionate world.

So, the next time you're in conversation, put away your distractions, make eye contact, and truly listen. You might be surprised at what you learn.

Now go forth and become a master of active listening!

ᑭᑭᑭ

FORTY-NINE

PRESENT SOLUTIONS RATHER THAN PROBLEMS—IT INSPIRES CONFIDENCE

Solutions, Not Complaints: The Power of Positive Action

Imagine walking into a room and immediately being bombarded with a litany of problems. "The traffic was terrible," "My coffee got cold," "The printer is jammed again!" It's enough to dampen anyone's spirits, isn't it?

Focusing on solutions, on the other hand, creates a more positive and productive atmosphere. It shifts the focus from negativity to possibility, inspiring action and encouraging collaboration.

The Power of Solution-Oriented Communication:

<u>Persuasion Supercharged</u>: When you present solutions instead of just problems, you become a more persuasive communicator. People are naturally drawn to those who offer hope and a path forward.

<u>Building Stronger Relationships</u>: Focusing on solutions fosters a more positive and collaborative environment. It shows that you're not just pointing out problems, but actively seeking solutions.

<u>Increased Motivation</u>: When you present solutions, you inspire others to take action and work towards a common goal.

<u>Boosting Confidence</u>: By focusing on solutions, you demonstrate a proactive and optimistic mindset, which can boost your own confidence and the confidence of those around you.

ᐅᐅᐅ

Tips for Focusing on Solutions:

Identify the Problem Clearly: Before proposing solutions, clearly define the problem at hand.

Brainstorm Possible Solutions: Encourage creative thinking and brainstorm a range of possible solutions.

Focus on Actionable Steps: Instead of just identifying problems, focus on concrete steps that can be taken to address those problems.

Be Open to Feedback and Collaboration: Be open to feedback from others and be willing to collaborate to find the best possible solutions.

ᐅᐅᐅ

Fun Fact:

The concept of "solution-focused therapy" is a popular approach in counseling and therapy. It focuses on identifying and amplifying existing strengths and resources to help individuals overcome challenges.

Reflection Questions:

How often do you find yourself dwelling on problems instead of focusing on solutions?

What are some situations where focusing on solutions would be particularly beneficial?

How can you cultivate a more solution-oriented mindset in your daily life?

Focusing on solutions is more than just being optimistic; it's a powerful approach to communication and problem-solving. By shifting your focus from problems to possibilities, you can create a more positive and productive environment, inspire action, and achieve greater success in all your endeavors.

So, the next time you encounter a challenge, remember to ask yourself, "What are some potential solutions?" You might be surprised at the creative and innovative ideas that emerge.

Now go forth and embrace the power of solution-focused thinking!

ᐅᐅᐅ

FIFTY

ANTICIPATE OBJECTIONS AND ADDRESS THEM CALMLY—IT REDUCES RESISTANCE

The Art of Pre-emption: Anticipating Objections for Smooth Sailing

Imagine trying to convince your friend to go hiking. They might say, "But I'm not in shape!" or "What if it rains?" These are common objections, and if you're not prepared, they can derail your plans faster than a sudden thunderstorm.

Anticipating objections is like having a roadmap for a successful conversation. It allows you to address potential roadblocks before they even arise, making your communication smoother, more persuasive, and more effective.

The Power of Proactive Objection Handling:

<u>Boosting Confidence</u>: When you're prepared for potential objections, you feel more confident and in control of the conversation.

<u>Increasing Persuasion</u>: By addressing objections proactively, you demonstrate that you've considered different viewpoints and that you have thoughtful responses.

<u>Building Trust</u>: Acknowledging and addressing potential concerns shows that you value the other person's perspective and are willing to work with them.

<u>Improving Negotiation</u>: In a negotiation, anticipating and addressing objections is crucial for reaching a mutually agreeable outcome.

ᗏᗏᗏ

Tips for Anticipating and Addressing Objections:

<u>Put on Your Thinking Cap</u>: Before presenting your ideas, take some time to brainstorm potential objections.

<u>Role-Play</u>: Practice your presentation with a friend or colleague and have them play the role of the "skeptic."

<u>Prepare Concise and Reassuring Responses</u>: Develop concise and persuasive responses to common objections.

<u>Acknowledge and Validate Concerns</u>: Even if you don't agree with the objection, acknowledge the other person's concerns and show that you understand their perspective.

ᗏᗏᗏ

Fun Fact: *Experienced negotiators often spend significant time anticipating potential objections and preparing their responses. This allows them to maintain their composure and navigate challenging conversations with confidence.*

Reflection Questions:

What are some common objections that you encounter in your daily interactions?

How can you better anticipate and address potential objections in your conversations?

How can anticipating objections help you to become a more persuasive and influential communicator?

Anticipating objections is like having a secret weapon in your communication arsenal. By proactively addressing potential roadblocks, you can navigate challenging conversations with confidence, build stronger relationships, and achieve your goals more effectively.

So, the next time you're preparing for a conversation, take a moment to put on your "objection anticipation" hat. You might be surprised at how much it can improve your communication skills.

Now go forth and conquer those objections!

ᗏᗏᗏ

FIFTY-ONE

USE POSITIVE REINFORCEMENT—IT ENCOURAGES COOPERATION

The Power of Positive Reinforcement: Rewarding Success, Fostering Cooperation

Imagine training a dog. You wouldn't punish them for barking, right? Instead, you'd reward them with treats and praise when they sit or stay. This is the essence of positive reinforcement – encouraging desired behaviors by rewarding them.

This principle isn't just for dogs; it's a powerful tool in human communication as well. By acknowledging and rewarding positive behavior, we can foster cooperation, build stronger relationships, and create a more positive and motivating environment.

The Magic of Positive Reinforcement:

<u>Boosting Motivation</u>: Positive reinforcement motivates people to repeat desired behaviors. When people feel appreciated and valued for their efforts, they're more likely to be motivated to continue.

<u>Building Confidence</u>: Receiving positive feedback boosts self-esteem and confidence. It helps people feel good about themselves and their abilities.

<u>Fostering Collaboration</u>: In a team setting, positive reinforcement encourages teamwork and collaboration. When individuals feel valued and appreciated for their contributions, they're more likely to work together

effectively.

Creating a Positive Environment: A culture of positive reinforcement creates a more enjoyable and motivating environment. It fosters a sense of camaraderie and encourages people to strive for excellence.

ᚦᚦᚦ

Tips for Using Positive Reinforcement Effectively:

Be Specific and Sincere: Instead of generic praise, be specific about what the person did well. For example, instead of saying "Good job," say "I really appreciate the way you communicated your ideas clearly and concisely."

Offer Genuine Praise: Make sure your praise is sincere and genuine. People can easily detect insincere flattery.

Acknowledge Effort: Acknowledge and appreciate effort, even if the outcome wasn't perfect.

Use a Variety of Reinforcements: Positive reinforcement can take many forms, such as verbal praise, public recognition, rewards, and opportunities for growth.

ᚦᚦᚦ

Fun Fact:

Positive reinforcement is a key principle in behavioral psychology, and it has been used effectively in various settings, from classrooms to workplaces to animal training.

Reflection Questions:

How often do you use positive reinforcement in your interactions with others?

What are some ways you can incorporate more positive reinforcement into your daily life?

How can positive reinforcement help you build stronger relationships and achieve your goals?

Positive reinforcement is a powerful tool for building stronger relationships, fostering motivation, and creating a more positive and productive environment. By acknowledging and rewarding positive behavior, we can encourage others to reach their full potential and create a more supportive and uplifting world.

So, the next time you have the opportunity, don't hesitate to offer a word of praise, a sincere thank you, or a small token of appreciation. You might be surprised at the positive impact it can have.

Now go forth and spread positivity!

ᗡᗡᗡ

FIFTY-TWO

SPEAK WITH CONVICTION—IT ENHANCES YOUR AUTHORITY

The Power of Conviction: Commanding Attention and Inspiring Action

Picture this: You're trying to persuade your team to adopt a new strategy. You present the facts, the figures, the logic... but something's missing. It's like trying to start a fire with damp wood – no spark, no flame.

Enter the power of conviction. Speaking with conviction isn't about shouting or being aggressive; it's about delivering your message with authenticity, passion, and a genuine belief in its importance.

The Magic of Speaking with Conviction:

<u>Persuasion Supercharged</u>: When you speak with conviction, your message carries more weight. People are more likely to be persuaded by someone who believes in their own words.

<u>Building Trust and Credibility</u>: Speaking with conviction demonstrates confidence and integrity. It shows that you believe in what you're saying and that you're willing to stand behind your ideas.

<u>Inspiring Action</u>: When you speak with passion and conviction, you inspire others to take action. Your enthusiasm is contagious and motivates others to get on board.

<u>Negotiation Advantage</u>: In a negotiation, speaking with conviction allows you to confidently state your position and advocate for your interests.

ᕤᕤᕤ

Tips for Speaking with Conviction:

<u>Believe in Your Message</u>: Genuinely believe in the importance of what you're communicating.

<u>Practice, Practice, Practice</u>: Rehearse your message beforehand to build confidence and fluency.

<u>Use Body Language</u>: Maintain good eye contact, use gestures effectively, and speak clearly and confidently.

<u>Modulate Your Voice</u>: Vary your tone and pace to keep your audience engaged.

ᕤᕤᕤ

Fun Fact:

Great public speakers, like Martin Luther King Jr. and Barack Obama, are masters of speaking with conviction. Their powerful speeches moved millions and inspired social change.

Reflection Questions:

How confident do you feel when expressing your opinions and ideas?

What are some situations where speaking with conviction is particularly important?

How can you improve your delivery to convey your message with more conviction?

Speaking with conviction is a powerful communication skill that can help you achieve your goals, build stronger relationships, and inspire others to action. So, the next time you need to communicate an important message, remember to speak with passion, authenticity, and unwavering belief.

Now go forth and let your voice be heard with conviction!

ᕤᕤᕤ

FIFTY-THREE

ACKNOWLEDGE OPPOSING VIEWS—IT SHOWS RESPECT AND BALANCE

The Art of Acknowledgment: Respecting Opposing Views

Imagine a world where everyone only listened to opinions that mirrored their own. Sounds pretty boring, right?

The beauty of human interaction lies in its diversity. We all have unique perspectives, experiences, and beliefs. Acknowledging opposing views, even when we disagree, is not just about being polite; it's about fostering understanding, building bridges, and creating a more informed and nuanced world.

The Power of Acknowledging Opposing Views:

Building Trust and Respect: When you acknowledge opposing views, you show that you value the other person's perspective and are willing to engage in a respectful dialogue.

Fostering Deeper Understanding: By considering different viewpoints, you gain a deeper understanding of the issue at hand. You can learn from others, identify potential weaknesses in your own arguments, and refine your own thinking.

Improving Decision-Making: When you consider all sides of an issue, you're more likely to make informed and well-rounded decisions.

<u>Creating a More Inclusive Society</u>: Acknowledging and respecting diverse perspectives fosters a more inclusive and tolerant society where everyone feels valued and heard.

ᗡᗡᗡ

Tips for Acknowledging Opposing Views:

<u>Active Listening</u>: Truly listen to the other person's perspective, even if you disagree with it.

<u>Summarize and Reflect</u>: Summarize their viewpoint to ensure you understand it correctly. For example, "So, if I understand correctly, your main concern is..."

<u>Find Common Ground</u>: Look for areas of agreement and shared values.

<u>Be Open to Changing Your Mind</u>: Be willing to reconsider your own position if presented with compelling evidence or arguments.

Fun Fact:

The ancient Greek philosopher Socrates was renowned for his use of the Socratic method, which involved asking probing questions to challenge assumptions and encourage critical thinking.

Reflection Questions:

How often do you actively listen to and consider opposing viewpoints?

What are some situations where acknowledging opposing views is particularly important?

How can you improve your ability to respectfully engage with those who hold different views?

Acknowledging opposing views is not about surrendering your own beliefs; it's about embracing the richness of human thought and engaging in meaningful dialogue. By respectfully considering different perspectives, we can learn and grow, build stronger relationships, and create a more informed and tolerant world.

So, the next time you encounter a differing viewpoint, take a deep breath, listen with an open mind, and remember that the exchange of ideas is a valuable and enriching experience.

ᗡᗡᗡ

FIFTY-FOUR

SHOW ENTHUSIASM—IT'S CONTAGIOUS AND MOTIVATES OTHERS

The Enthusiasm Epidemic: How Passion Fuels Connection

Imagine trying to convince your friend to go on a road trip with you. You could say, "We should probably go on a road trip sometime soon." Or, you could say, "I'm SO excited about this potential road trip! Imagine the freedom of the open road, the amazing food we'll discover, and the hilarious adventures we'll have along the way!"

Feel the difference? Enthusiasm is contagious. It's like adding a spark to the kindling, igniting excitement and motivation in others.

The Magic of Enthusiasm:

<u>Persuasion Powerhouse</u>: Enthusiasm is incredibly persuasive. When you're genuinely excited about something, others are more likely to be drawn in and share your excitement.

<u>Building Stronger Connections</u>: Enthusiasm is infectious. When you're enthusiastic about something, it makes others feel more engaged and connected to you.

<u>Fostering Collaboration</u>: Enthusiasm is a powerful motivator. When you're enthusiastic about a project, it inspires others to join in and contribute their own energy and ideas.

<u>Increasing Creativity and Innovation</u>: Enthusiasm unlocks creativity. When you're excited about something, you're more likely to think outside the box, come up with innovative solutions, and approach challenges with a positive and optimistic mindset.

ᕔᕔᕔ

Tips for Cultivating and Communicating Enthusiasm:

<u>Find Your Passion</u>: Identify your passions and pursue them with enthusiasm.

<u>Practice Positive Self-Talk</u>: Use positive affirmations and self-talk to cultivate a more enthusiastic mindset.

<u>Use Body Language</u>: Express your enthusiasm through your body language. Smile, use expressive gestures, and maintain good eye contact.

<u>Share Your Excitement with Others</u>: Don't keep your enthusiasm bottled up! Share it with the world and inspire others to join you.

Fun Fact:

Studies have shown that enthusiastic individuals are often perceived as more competent, trustworthy, and likable.

Reflection Questions:

What are you most enthusiastic about in your life right now?

How can you more effectively communicate your enthusiasm to others?

How can you use your enthusiasm to inspire and motivate those around you?

Enthusiasm is contagious. It's a powerful force that can ignite passion, inspire action, and build stronger connections. So, let your enthusiasm shine! Embrace your passions, share your excitement with the world, and watch as your enthusiasm inspires others to join you on your journey.

Now go forth and spread the enthusiasm! The world needs a little more sparkle.

ᕔᕔᕔ

FIFTY-FIVE

APPEAL TO EMOTIONS—IT DRIVES DECISIONS MORE THAN LOGIC

The Heart of the Matter: Why Emotions Rule the Day

We like to think we're all rational beings, making decisions based on logic and reason. But let's be honest, our emotions often play a much bigger role than we realize. Think about your favorite movie. Was it the flawless plot or the way it made you laugh, cry, or feel deeply connected to the characters that truly won you over?

Appealing to emotions is a powerful tool in communication. It taps into our deepest desires, fears, and hopes, making your message more compelling and persuasive.

The Emotional Advantage:

Persuasion Supercharged: When you connect with someone's emotions, you're more likely to persuade them. Emotions like fear, joy, hope, and empathy can drive action more powerfully than any logical argument.

Building Deeper Connections: Appealing to emotions creates a stronger emotional connection with your audience. It allows them to feel the impact of your message on a deeper level.

Storytelling Powerhouse: Storytelling is all about evoking emotions. By crafting stories that resonate with your audience's feelings, you can make your message more engaging, memorable, and impactful.

Negotiation Edge: Understanding and appealing to the emotions of the other party can help you find common ground and reach mutually beneficial agreements.

ᐅᐅᐅ

Tips for Appealing to Emotions:
Tell Stories: Use stories to illustrate your points and connect with your audience on an emotional level.

Use Vivid Language: Paint a picture with your words. Use sensory details and emotional language to evoke feelings in your audience.

Appeal to Values: Connect your message to the audience's values and beliefs.

Be Authentic: Be genuine and authentic in your communication. Let your own passion and enthusiasm shine through.

ᐅᐅᐅ

Fun Fact:
Many successful marketing campaigns rely heavily on emotional appeals. Think of heartwarming commercials that tug at your heartstrings or advertisements that tap into your desire for status or belonging.

Reflection Questions:
How do emotions influence your own decision-making?

What are some examples of how you've seen emotions used effectively in advertising or marketing?

How can you use emotional appeals more effectively in your own communication?

While logic and reason play important roles in communication, let's not underestimate the power of emotions. By understanding and appealing to the emotions of your audience, you can create more persuasive, engaging, and impactful communication.

So, the next time you're trying to persuade someone, remember to tap into the power of emotions. Tell a story, evoke feelings, and connect with them on a deeper level.

ᐅᐅᐅ

FIFTY-SIX

SHARE RELATABLE EXAMPLES—IT CREATES A PERSONAL CONNECTION

The Relatability Factor: Connecting Through Shared Experiences

Have you ever been in a conversation where someone starts talking about abstract concepts and you feel completely lost? It's like they're speaking a different language!

That's where the power of relatable examples comes in. By sharing personal anecdotes, real-life situations, or familiar experiences, you create a bridge of understanding between yourself and your audience.

The Magic of Relatability:

<u>Persuasion Supercharged</u>: When you use relatable examples, your message becomes more engaging and persuasive. People are more likely to be convinced by something they can personally relate to.

<u>Building Deeper Connections</u>: Sharing relatable experiences fosters a sense of connection and common ground. It shows that you understand the other person's perspective and that you share similar experiences.

<u>Increasing Trust and Credibility</u>: Using relatable examples makes you seem more authentic and approachable. It shows that you're not just talking theory; you're speaking from experience.

<u>Making Complex Ideas Easier to Understand</u>: Relatable examples can help to simplify complex ideas and make them more accessible to your

audience.

᛫᛫᛫

Tips for Using Relatable Examples:

<u>Draw from Your Own Experiences</u>: Share personal anecdotes and real-life experiences to illustrate your points.

<u>Use Everyday Examples</u>: Draw on common experiences that everyone can relate to, such as traffic jams, grocery shopping, or waiting in line.

<u>Use Metaphors and Analogies</u>: Metaphors and analogies can help you explain complex ideas by comparing them to familiar concepts.

<u>Pay Attention to Your Audience</u>: Tailor your examples to your audience and their interests.

᛫᛫᛫

Fun Fact:

Great storytellers, from novelists to comedians, are masters of using relatable examples to connect with their audience. They weave personal anecdotes and everyday experiences into their narratives to create a sense of shared humanity.

Reflection Questions:

How often do you use relatable examples in your conversations?

What are some situations where using relatable examples would be particularly beneficial?

How can you improve your ability to find and share relatable examples in your communication?

Relatability is the key to connecting with your audience on a deeper level. By sharing personal anecdotes, using everyday examples, and drawing on shared experiences, you can make your message more engaging, persuasive, and impactful.

So, the next time you're communicating, remember to sprinkle in some relatable examples. You might be surprised at how much it enhances your connection with your audience and strengthens your communication.

Now go forth and share your stories! The world is waiting to hear them.

᛫᛫᛫

FIFTY-SEVEN

CREATE A SENSE OF URGENCY—IT SPURS ACTION

The Urgency Factor: Igniting Action with a Spark

Imagine a fire alarm blaring. Suddenly, everyone springs into action. Why? Because it signals immediate danger, creating a sense of urgency.

Urgency, while often associated with stress, can also be a powerful tool for positive change. When you communicate with a sense of urgency, you motivate others to act, sparking action and driving them towards a common goal.

The Power of Urgency:

<u>Persuasion Supercharged</u>: Creating a sense of urgency makes your message more compelling and persuasive. People are more likely to take action when they feel a sense of urgency or a fear of missing out.

<u>Driving Action</u>: Urgency motivates people to act quickly and decisively. It helps to overcome procrastination and get things done.

<u>Negotiation Advantage</u>: In a negotiation, a sense of urgency can help you reach a quicker agreement. For example, highlighting time constraints or limited availability can encourage the other party to move forward.

<u>Storytelling Spark</u>: Creating a sense of urgency can make your stories more engaging. It builds suspense and keeps your audience on the edge of their seats.

<p>

Tips for Creating a Sense of Urgency:

<u>Highlight Time Constraints</u>: Clearly communicate deadlines and timelines. For example, "This offer is only available for a limited time."

<u>Emphasize the Consequences of Inaction</u>: Explain the potential negative consequences of delaying action.

<u>Use Vivid Language</u>: Paint a picture of the potential rewards or the potential risks associated with inaction.

<u>Create a Sense of Competition</u>: If appropriate, create a sense of competition or scarcity to motivate action.

ᗐᗐᗐ

Fun Fact:

Many successful marketing campaigns rely on creating a sense of urgency. Limited-time offers, flash sales, and scarcity marketing are all tactics designed to motivate immediate action.

Reflection Questions:

How do you typically create a sense of urgency in your communication?

What are some situations where creating a sense of urgency is appropriate and ethical?

How can you use urgency effectively to motivate yourself and others to achieve their goals?

Creating a sense of urgency is a powerful communication tool that can drive action, motivate change, and achieve remarkable results. By strategically communicating the importance of timely action, you can inspire others to seize the moment and achieve their goals.

So, the next time you need to motivate someone, remember the power of urgency. Ignite the spark and watch them take action!

ᗐᗐᗐ

FIFTY-EIGHT

BE ADAPTABLE—FLEXIBILITY MAKES YOUR INFLUENCE MORE EFFECTIVE

Bend Like a Reed: The Power of Adaptability in Influence

Imagine trying to navigate a crowded marketplace. If you stubbornly stick to one path and refuse to adjust your course, you're likely to get stuck or even bumped into someone. But if you're adaptable, you can weave through the crowds, find new routes, and reach your destination with ease.

Adaptability is like that – it allows you to navigate the ever-changing landscape of human interaction with grace and effectiveness.

The Magic of Adaptability:

Persuasion Powerhouse: When you're adaptable, you can adjust your approach to suit the specific needs and preferences of your audience. This makes your message more resonant and increases your chances of persuasion.

Building Stronger Relationships: Adaptability fosters stronger relationships by demonstrating respect and understanding for the other person's perspective. It shows that you're willing to adjust your approach to find common ground.

<u>Negotiation Ninja</u>: In a negotiation, adaptability is crucial. Being able to adjust your position, explore alternative solutions, and find creative compromises is key to reaching a mutually beneficial agreement.

<u>Storytelling Mastery</u>: Adaptable storytellers can adjust their narratives to suit the interests and preferences of their audience, making their stories more engaging and impactful.

ᠥᠥᠥ

Tips for Cultivating Adaptability:

<u>Active Listening</u>: Pay close attention to the other person's verbal and non-verbal cues. Are they receptive to your message? Do they seem confused or disengaged?

<u>Be Open to Feedback</u>: Be receptive to feedback and be willing to adjust your approach based on the other person's reactions.

<u>Embrace Change</u>: Embrace change as an opportunity for growth and learning.

Develop Your "Spidey Sense" for Social Cues: Pay attention to social cues and adjust your communication style accordingly.

ᠥᠥᠥ

Fun Fact:

The ancient Chinese philosophy of "Wu Wei" emphasizes the importance of going with the flow and adapting to changing circumstances. It suggests that by yielding to the natural course of events, we can achieve greater harmony and success.

How adaptable are you in your communication style?

What are some situations where you've had to adapt your approach to be more effective?

How can you cultivate more adaptability in your interactions with others?

In a world of constant change, adaptability is not just a skill, it's a superpower. By embracing flexibility, adjusting your approach, and navigating the ever-changing currents of human interaction, you can become a more effective communicator, build stronger relationships, and achieve your goals with greater ease.

So, the next time you're faced with a communication challenge, remember to be like a reed in the wind – bend, but don't break. Adapt, adjust, and find a way to reach your destination.

❧❧❧

FIFTY-NINE

USE VISUALS TO REINFORCE YOUR MESSAGE—THEY BOOST RETENTION

A Picture is Worth a Thousand Words: The Power of Visuals in Communication

Let's be honest, sometimes words just aren't enough. That's where the power of visuals comes in. Whether it's a captivating image, a simple diagram, or a short video, visuals have an incredible ability to grab attention, convey information, and leave a lasting impact.

The Magic of Visual Communication:

<u>Persuasion Supercharged</u>: Visuals can make your message more persuasive and memorable. They can evoke emotions, tell stories, and make complex ideas easier to understand.

<u>Boosting Engagement</u>: Visuals are attention-grabbers. They break up text, making your message more engaging and easier to read.

<u>Improving Retention</u>: Studies have shown that people are more likely to remember information when it's presented visually.

<u>Storytelling Made Spectacular</u>: Visuals bring stories to life. They add depth and richness to your narratives, making them more immersive and engaging.

ᐅᐅᐅ

Tips for Using Visuals Effectively:

Choose the Right Visuals: Select visuals that are relevant, high-quality, and easy to understand.

Keep it Simple: Avoid cluttering your message with too many visuals. Choose visuals that are clear, concise, and easy to interpret.

Tell a Story with Your Visuals: Use visuals to illustrate your points, tell a story, or evoke emotions.

Use Visuals Sparingly: Don't overload your audience with visuals. Use them strategically to enhance your message, not overwhelm it.

ᐳᐳᐳ

Fun Fact:

The human brain processes visual information much faster than text. In fact, we can process visual information up to 60,000 times faster than text.

Reflection Questions:

How often do you use visuals in your communication?

What are some examples of how you can incorporate visuals into your presentations, reports, or even casual conversations?

How can you use visuals more effectively to enhance your communication and influence?

In today's visually driven world, the power of visuals cannot be underestimated. By incorporating visuals into your communication, you can make your message more engaging, persuasive, and memorable. So, the next time you're trying to communicate an idea, ask yourself, "How can I enhance this message with a visual?" You might be surprised at the impact it can have.

Now go forth and unleash the power of visual communication!

ᐳᐳᐳ

SIXTY

ASK THOUGHT-PROVOKING QUESTIONS—IT STIMULATES ENGAGEMENT.

The Question Mark Revolution: Unlocking Deeper Conversations

Imagine a conversation where everyone just nods and agrees. Sounds a bit dull, doesn't it? That's where the magic of thought-provoking questions comes in. They're like sparks that ignite deeper conversations, encourage critical thinking, and unlock a world of new ideas.

The Power of Thought-Provoking Questions:

Persuasion Supercharged: By asking thought-provoking questions, you can subtly guide the conversation in a direction that supports your perspective. You encourage others to consider different viewpoints and ultimately arrive at a conclusion that aligns with your own.

Storytelling Catalyst: Thought-provoking questions can transform a simple story into a captivating journey of exploration. They encourage listeners to delve deeper, analyze the themes, and connect the story to their own experiences.

Negotiation Ninja: In a negotiation, thoughtful questions can help you understand the other party's needs and concerns, uncover hidden interests, and identify areas of common ground.

Building Deeper Connections: Thought-provoking questions encourage deeper engagement and create a more meaningful conversation. They show that you value the other person's thoughts and opinions and are genuinely interested in their perspective.

ϷϷϷ

Tips for Crafting Thought-Provoking Questions:

Go Beyond the Surface: Avoid yes/no questions. Instead, ask questions that require deeper reflection and analysis. For example, instead of asking "Do you like this movie?", ask "What were the most memorable aspects of this movie for you?"

Encourage Critical Thinking: Ask questions that challenge assumptions and encourage deeper analysis. For example, "What are the potential consequences of this decision?"

Use "What if...?" Scenarios: Explore different possibilities by asking "what if" questions. For example, "What if we approached this problem from a different angle?"

Listen Actively: Pay close attention to their responses and use their answers to formulate further thought-provoking questions.

ϷϷϷ

Fun Fact:

The Socratic method, a famous method of inquiry, relies heavily on the use of thought-provoking questions to guide students towards deeper understanding and critical thinking.

Reflection Questions:

How often do you use thought-provoking questions in your conversations?

What are some examples of thought-provoking questions you could use in your next conversation?

How can you use thought-provoking questions to improve your communication skills in various settings (work, social, family)?

Thought-provoking questions are the keys to unlocking deeper conversations, stimulating critical thinking, and fostering a more engaging and insightful communication experience. So, the next time you're in conversation, ditch the mundane questions and embrace the power of the thought-provoking query. You might be surprised at the fascinating discussions that unfold.

Now go forth and ignite the sparks of conversation with your insightful questions!

☙☙☙

SIXTY-ONE

HIGHLIGHT LONG-TERM BENEFITS—IT SHIFTS FOCUS BEYOND IMMEDIATE RESULTS

Beyond the Immediate: The Power of Long-Term Vision

Imagine you're trying to convince someone to start exercising. You could say, "You'll feel better in the moment." But what if you said, "Imagine waking up feeling energized every day, having more energy to play with your kids, and significantly reducing your risk of serious health problems down the line."

See the difference? Focusing on long-term benefits shifts the perspective from immediate gratification to sustained well-being. It's like planting a seed and nurturing it, knowing that it will blossom into something beautiful and rewarding.

The Power of Long-Term Vision:

Persuasion Supercharged: Highlighting long-term benefits taps into people's deeper motivations and aspirations. It resonates with their values and encourages them to make choices that will have a lasting positive impact.

<u>Building Stronger Commitments</u>: When people understand the long-term benefits of a decision, they're more likely to be committed to that decision and persevere through challenges.

<u>Fostering Sustainable Change</u>: Focusing on long-term benefits encourages sustainable change. It shifts the focus from quick fixes to long-term solutions that have a lasting impact.

<u>Negotiation Advantage</u>: In a negotiation, highlighting the long-term benefits of a particular agreement can help you reach a mutually beneficial outcome that addresses the long-term interests of all parties.

ϷϷϷ

Tips for Highlighting Long-Term Benefits:

<u>Paint a Vivid Picture</u>: Use vivid language and storytelling to paint a picture of the future benefits.

<u>Use "If-Then" Statements</u>: For example, "If we implement this strategy, then we can expect to see..."

<u>Appeal to Values</u>: Connect the long-term benefits to the listener's values and aspirations.

<u>Be Patient</u>: It may take time for people to fully appreciate the long-term benefits of a particular decision.

ϷϷϷ

Fun Fact:

The concept of delayed gratification, the ability to resist immediate rewards in favor of larger, long-term rewards, is a key predictor of success in various areas of life.

Reflection Questions:

How often do you focus on long-term benefits in your communication?

What are some situations where highlighting long-term benefits would be particularly effective?

How can you cultivate a more long-term perspective in your own decision-making?

Focusing on long-term benefits is not just about delayed gratification; it's about investing in a better future. By highlighting the long-term rewards of your ideas and actions, you can inspire others, build stronger relationships, and create a more positive and sustainable future for all.

So, the next time you're communicating, remember to look beyond the immediate and consider the long-term implications of your words and actions.

Now go forth and plant the seeds for a brighter future!

❦❦❦

SIXTY-TWO

SPEAK THEIR LANGUAGE—ADAPT TO THEIR COMMUNICATION STYLE

Speaking Their Language: The Art of Communication Chameleon

Imagine trying to explain a complex technical concept to a five-year-old. You'd use simple words, maybe even tell a story, right? That's the essence of adapting your communication style. It's about understanding your audience and tailoring your message to their unique needs and preferences.

The Magic of Communication Chameleonism:

<u>Persuasion Supercharged</u>: When you speak their language, you immediately build rapport and increase your credibility. People are more receptive to messages that are presented in a way they can easily understand and relate to.

<u>Building Stronger Connections</u>: Adapting your communication style shows that you value the other person and are willing to make an effort to connect with them on their level. This fosters stronger relationships and builds trust.

<u>Negotiation Ninja</u>: In a negotiation, adapting your communication style can help you build rapport with the other party and find common ground.

By understanding their communication style, you can adjust your approach to make the negotiation more productive and successful.

Storytelling Mastery: Effective storytelling requires adapting your style to your audience. You need to choose the right tone, vocabulary, and level of detail to keep your audience engaged and captivated.

ƤƤƤ

Tips for Becoming a Communication Chameleon:

Observe and Analyze: Pay close attention to the other person's communication style. How do they express themselves? What kind of language do they use? What are their communication preferences?

Adjust Your Tone and Vocabulary: Adjust your tone of voice, word choice, and pace to match the other person's communication style.

Use Visual Aids: If appropriate, use visuals like diagrams, charts, or videos to help illustrate your points and make your message more engaging.

Practice Active Listening: Pay close attention to the other person's responses and adjust your communication style accordingly.

ƤƤƤ

Fun Fact:

Great salespeople are masters of adapting their communication style to the needs and preferences of their customers. They can seamlessly switch between different styles to build rapport, build trust, and close the deal.

Reflection Questions:

How well do you adapt your communication style to different audiences?

What are some situations where adapting your communication style is particularly important?

How can you improve your ability to understand and adapt to different communication styles?

Being a communication chameleon is not about being insincere. It's about demonstrating respect, understanding, and a genuine desire to connect with others on their level. By adapting your communication style to your audience, you can build stronger relationships, enhance your influence, and achieve your communication goals with greater ease.

So, the next time you're in conversation, remember to put on your communication chameleon hat and adapt your approach to the unique needs and preferences of your audience. You might be surprised at how much it improves your interactions.

❦❦❦

SIXTY-THREE

PROVIDE STEP-BY-STEP GUIDANCE—IT ENSURES CLARITY AND ACTION

The Roadmap to Success: The Power of Step-by-Step Guidance

Imagine trying to bake a cake without a recipe. You might have the ingredients, but without clear instructions, you're likely to end up with a culinary disaster.

Similarly, when communicating complex ideas, providing step-by-step guidance is crucial. It breaks down overwhelming information into manageable chunks, making it easier for your audience to understand, engage, and take action.

The Magic of Step-by-Step Guidance:

<u>Persuasion Supercharged</u>: When you provide clear steps, you empower your audience to take action. It reduces the feeling of being overwhelmed and makes the desired outcome seem more achievable.

<u>Building Trust and Credibility</u>: By providing clear and concise instructions, you demonstrate your expertise and build trust with your audience.

<u>Improving Understanding</u>: Breaking down complex information into smaller, more digestible steps enhances comprehension and reduces confusion.

<u>Fostering Action and Achievement</u>: Clear step-by-step guidance provides a roadmap for success, motivating people to take action and achieve their goals.

ƿƿƿ

Tips for Providing Effective Step-by-Step Guidance:

<u>Keep it Concise and Clear</u>: Use simple language and avoid jargon. Each step should be concise and easy to understand.

<u>Use Numbers or Bullet Points</u>: Numbered lists or bullet points make it easy to follow the sequence of steps.

<u>Provide Visual Aids</u>: Use diagrams, flowcharts, or checklists to illustrate the steps visually.

<u>Offer Support and Encouragement</u>: Encourage your audience to take action and provide support along the way.

ƿƿƿ

Fun Fact:

The concept of "chunking" information, breaking down large pieces of information into smaller, more manageable chunks, is a powerful learning technique used by educators and cognitive psychologists.

Reflection Questions:

How often do you provide step-by-step guidance in your communication?

What are some situations where providing step-by-step guidance would be particularly beneficial?

How can you improve your ability to break down complex information into clear and concise steps?

Providing clear and concise step-by-step guidance is essential for effective communication. By breaking down complex information into manageable chunks, you empower your audience to understand, act, and achieve their goals.

So, the next time you're communicating a complex idea, remember to provide a clear roadmap to success. Guide your audience through the process, step-by-step, and watch them achieve their goals with confidence.

Now go forth and empower others with the gift of clear and concise guidance!

ƿƿƿ

SIXTY-FOUR

USE DATA SPARINGLY—IT ADDS CREDIBILITY WITHOUT OVERWHELMING

Data Detox: The Power of Less is More

Imagine trying to explain the deliciousness of a pizza by reciting the entire nutritional breakdown. You'd likely lose your audience before they even got to the part about the gooey cheese!

Data is powerful, but like spices in a dish, it's best used sparingly. Overwhelming your audience with numbers and figures can be as off-putting as a dish with too much salt.

The Magic of Data Sparsity:

<u>Persuasion Supercharged</u>: A few well-chosen data points can significantly enhance your persuasion. They lend credibility to your claims and make your arguments more convincing.

<u>Building Trust and Credibility</u>: Using data demonstrates that you've done your research and that you're presenting information that is accurate and reliable.

<u>Improving Clarity</u>: When used judiciously, data can clarify complex issues and help your audience understand the bigger picture.

<u>Avoiding Information Overload</u>: Overloading your audience with data can be overwhelming and counterproductive. By using data sparingly, you maintain their attention and keep your message focused.

ᚦᚦᚦ

Tips for Using Data Effectively:

Choose the Right Data: Select data that is relevant, reliable, and easy to understand.

Visualize Your Data: Use charts, graphs, or infographics to present data in a visually appealing and easy-to-digest format.

Tell a Story with Your Data: Don't just present data; use it to tell a story and illustrate your point.

Focus on Key Takeaways: Highlight the most important data points and avoid overwhelming your audience with unnecessary information.

ᚦᚦᚦ

Fun Fact:

The famous data visualization expert Hans Rosling was a master of using data to tell compelling stories. He used interactive visualizations and engaging storytelling to communicate complex global development issues in a clear and captivating way.

Reflection Questions:

How often do you use data to support your claims?

Do you tend to use too much data or too little?

How can you use data more effectively to enhance your communication and influence?

Data is a powerful tool, but like any powerful tool, it must be used wisely. By using data sparingly and strategically, you can enhance your communication, build trust, and effectively persuade your audience.

So, the next time you're tempted to bombard your audience with data, remember the power of less is more. Choose your data carefully, present it effectively, and let it speak volumes.

Now go forth and wield the power of data with finesse!

ᚦᚦᚦ

SIXTY-FIVE

BE CONSISTENT IN YOUR MESSAGE—IT BUILDS TRUST

Keeping Your Word: The Power of Consistency in Communication

Imagine a friend who always promises to call but rarely does. How would that make you feel? Probably a bit frustrated and maybe even a little hurt.

Consistency in communication is like building a sturdy bridge – it requires a solid foundation and unwavering support. When you consistently deliver on your promises and maintain a consistent message, you build trust and strengthen your relationships.

The Magic of Consistency:

<u>Persuasion Supercharged</u>: Consistency makes your message more believable and persuasive. When you consistently deliver on your promises, people are more likely to trust your words and be receptive to your ideas.

<u>Building Trust and Credibility</u>: Consistency is the cornerstone of trust. When you consistently act in accordance with your words and values, you build credibility and earn the respect of others.

<u>Fostering Reliability</u>: Consistency makes you a reliable source of information and support. People know that they can count on you to be consistent in your words and actions.

<u>Negotiation Ninja</u>: In negotiation, consistency is key. By maintaining a consistent position and sticking to your core values, you demonstrate strength and resolve, which can help you achieve a more favorable outcome.

♥♥♥

Tips for Maintaining Consistency in Communication:

<u>Think Before You Speak</u>: Before making a promise or stating an opinion, carefully consider the implications and ensure that you can consistently uphold your position.

<u>Be Mindful of Your Actions:</u> Ensure that your actions align with your words.

<u>Review and Refine</u>: Regularly review your communication style and identify areas where you can improve consistency.

<u>Be Honest and Transparent</u>: If you need to adjust your position, be honest and transparent with others. Explain the reasons for the change and maintain open communication.

ppp

Fun Fact:

Brand consistency is a key factor in successful marketing. Companies that consistently deliver on their brand promise build stronger brand loyalty and customer relationships.

Reflection Questions:

How consistent are you in your communication?

Are there any areas where you could improve your consistency in communication?

How can maintaining consistency in your communication help you build stronger relationships and achieve your goals?

Consistency is the cornerstone of effective communication. By consistently delivering on your promises, maintaining a consistent message, and acting in accordance with your values, you build trust, credibility, and stronger relationships.

So, the next time you communicate, remember the importance of consistency. Be mindful of your words and actions, and strive to build a reputation for reliability and integrity.

Now go forth and communicate with consistency and confidence!

ppp

SIXTY-SIX

ALIGN YOUR BODY LANGUAGE WITH YOUR WORDS—IT AVOIDS MIXED SIGNALS

The Body Language Blueprint: Aligning Words and Actions

Imagine trying to convince someone that you're excited about a new project, but you're slouching in your chair, avoiding eye contact, and sighing dramatically. Confused? You bet! Your body language is screaming "I'm bored!" while your words say "I'm enthusiastic!"

When your words and body language are mismatched, it's like a traffic jam where the signals are all pointing in different directions – nobody knows where to go!

The Magic of Alignment:

<u>Persuasion Powerhouse</u>: When your words and body language are aligned, your message becomes more powerful and impactful. It creates a sense of authenticity and builds trust with your audience. Imagine a passionate speaker who leans forward, makes eye contact, and uses gestures to emphasize their points. Their enthusiasm is contagious!

<u>Building Rapport and Connection</u>: Aligned body language fosters stronger connections. It shows that you're engaged, present, and genuinely interested in the conversation. Mirroring (subtly mimicking their posture and gestures) can help you build rapport and create a sense of connection, making the other person feel more comfortable and understood.

<u>Negotiation Advantage</u>: In a negotiation, aligned body language conveys confidence and assertiveness. A firm handshake, direct eye contact, and an upright posture can help you maintain a strong presence and effectively communicate your position.

<u>Storytelling Mastery</u>: Aligned body language brings your stories to life. If you're describing a thrilling adventure, your gestures should be dynamic and energetic. If you're sharing a poignant memory, your tone and body language should reflect the emotion of the moment.

ᗷᗷᗷ

Tips for Aligning Your Words and Actions:

<u>Become a Body Language Observer</u>: Pay close attention to your own body language and the body language of others. How does your posture, facial expressions, and gestures affect your communication?

<u>Practice in Front of a Mirror</u>: Rehearse presentations or important conversations in front of a mirror to become more aware of your body language and how it impacts your message.

<u>Record Yourself</u>: Record yourself speaking and then analyze your video. Are your words and actions aligned? Are you making effective use of body language?

<u>Seek Feedback</u>: Ask trusted friends or colleagues for feedback on your body language and communication style.

ᗷᗷᗷ

Fun Fact:

Studies have shown that body language can account for up to 93% of communication!

Reflection Questions:

How aware are you of your own body language?

What are some situations where your words and body language might be sending mixed signals?

How can you improve the alignment between your words and body language to enhance your communication and influence?

Aligning your words and body language is crucial for effective communication. It builds trust, enhances your credibility, and ensures that your message is received clearly and accurately.

So, the next time you're communicating, become mindful of your body language. Use it to enhance your message, build rapport, and leave a lasting impression.

Now go forth and communicate with confidence and grace!

❦❦❦

SIXTY-SEVEN

REINFORCE KEY POINTS WITH REPETITION—IT SOLIDIFIES UNDERSTANDING.

The Echo Chamber: Why Repetition is Your Brain's Best Friend (and How to Use It)

Hey there, fellow learner! Ever felt like you've studied something, but it just... poof... vanished from your memory? You're not alone. Our brains are amazing, but they're also a bit forgetful. That's where the magic of repetition comes in.

Think of your brain like a muscle. The more you work it out (in this case, by repeating information), the stronger it gets. Repetition isn't just about rote memorization; it's about deepening your understanding and making those juicy concepts stick.

Ways to Influence Your Brain (and Make Learning Stickier Than Glue)

The "Spaced Repetition" Trick: Don't cram! Review information at increasing intervals. For example, review a new concept today, again tomorrow, then in 3 days, then in a week, and so on. This tricks your brain into remembering the info for the long haul.

<u>Teach It Back</u>: Explain the concept to someone else, even if it's your dog (they're excellent listeners, trust me). Teaching forces you to organize your thoughts and identify any gaps in your understanding.

<u>The "Retrieval Practice" Power-Up</u>: Test yourself! Quiz yourself, use flashcards, or try to recall information without looking at your notes. This strengthens the neural pathways and makes it easier to access information when you need it.

<u>Turn it into a Story</u>: Humans are wired for stories. Weave the information into a narrative, a poem, or even a song. This makes learning more engaging and memorable.

<u>The "Multi-Sensory" Experience</u>: Engage all your senses! Draw diagrams, read aloud, listen to audio recordings, or even act out the concepts. The more senses you involve, the stronger the memory.

🎵🎵🎵

Let's Get Practical!

Imagine you're learning a new language. Instead of just reading the vocabulary list once, try this:

Day 1: Read the list, then try to write it down from memory.

Day 2: Review the list, then try to use the words in simple sentences.

Day 3: Teach the words to a friend (or your imaginary friend).

Day 4: Create flashcards and test yourself.

Day 5: Listen to a song in that language and try to pick out the words you've learned.

Studying for an exam? Don't just reread your notes.

Summarize key concepts in your own words.

Teach the material to a study buddy.

Create a mind map to visually connect different ideas.

Take practice quizzes under timed conditions.

Reward yourself for each successful study session!

Fun Facts to Fuel Your Brain

Did you know that sleep is crucial for memory consolidation? When you sleep, your brain replays the day's events, strengthening the neural connections.

Studies have shown that handwriting notes can actually improve learning and memory compared to typing.

Laughter can boost memory and cognitive function. So, don't be afraid to have some fun while you're learning!

🎵🎵🎵

Time for Some Self-Reflection

What's your biggest learning challenge?

How can you incorporate repetition into your current learning strategies?

What's one thing you'll try this week to make learning more engaging and effective?

Actionable Insights to Level Up Your Learning

Embrace the "spaced repetition" principle. Use apps like Anki or Memrise to schedule your reviews.

Find a learning buddy. Teaching someone else can solidify your own understanding.

Make learning fun! Turn it into a game, listen to music, or reward yourself for your efforts.

Remember: Learning is a journey, not a race. Be patient with yourself, celebrate your successes, and enjoy the process!

Now go forth and conquer!

If you're still struggling to remember something, try this: think about the last time you felt truly happy. Studies have shown that positive emotions can enhance memory recall.

ԲԲԲ

SIXTY-EIGHT

BUILD SUSPENSE BEFORE REVEALING A KEY IDEA—IT KEEPS ATTENTION

Hook 'Em & Hold 'Em: The Power of Suspense

Hey there, fellow wordsmiths! Let's talk about the art of storytelling. You know that feeling when you're reading a mystery, and every page leaves you hanging? That's suspense in action!

Why Suspense Matters:

Think of suspense as a powerful magnet. It draws your reader in, keeps them glued to the page, and makes them crave more. It's like a delicious meal – you savor each bite, anticipating the next flavor explosion.

Ways to Influence Your Audience with Suspense:

The Mysterious "What If?"

Example: "The old woman sat alone in the rocking chair, a single tear rolling down her cheek. What terrible secret did she hold?" This leaves the reader wondering: What's the secret? What made her cry?

The Ticking Clock:

Example: "The bomb was set to explode in 30 minutes. Could they find the defusal code in time?" This creates urgency and keeps readers on the edge of their seats.

The Unexpected Twist:

Example: "He thought he knew his best friend, but then he discovered a shocking truth about their shared past." This keeps readers guessing and makes them question everything they thought they knew.

The Cliffhanger:

Example: "Just as she reached for the doorknob, a shadow emerged from the darkness. The door creaked open..." This leaves the reader hanging, desperate to know what happens next.

The Use of Foreshadowing:

Example: "The raven croaked ominously in the treetops, a chilling reminder of the impending doom." Foreshadowing hints at future events, creating a sense of dread and anticipation.

ᚦᚦᚦ

Let's Get Practical!

The "What If" Game:

Exercise: Write a short sentence or phrase that sparks curiosity. For example: "The letter arrived unexpectedly." Now, brainstorm five "What If" questions based on this sentence. (What if the letter contained bad news? What if it was from a long-lost relative? What if it held the key to a hidden treasure?)

The "Ticking Clock" Challenge:

Exercise: Choose a simple scenario (e.g., getting ready for school, waiting for a bus). Now, add a time constraint to create urgency (e.g., "The bus leaves in 5 minutes," or "The test starts in 10 minutes"). Write a short paragraph describing the scene, highlighting the pressure of the time limit.

The "Twist" It Up:

Exercise: Take a familiar story (like a classic fairy tale). Now, give it an unexpected twist. For example: "Cinderella's glass slipper shatters, revealing a secret message inside."

ᚦᚦᚦ

Fun Facts:

Did you know that Alfred Hitchcock, the master of suspense, often used long takes and minimal music to build tension?

The term "cliffhanger" originated in early silent films, where a thrilling scene would literally end on a cliff!

Reflect on This:

How do you use suspense in your own life? (When telling stories, playing games, etc.)

What are some of your favorite suspenseful movies, books, or TV shows? Why do they keep you hooked?

How can you use suspense to make your writing more engaging and memorable?

Actionable Insights:

Start with a Hook: Grab your reader's attention from the very first sentence.

Build Gradually: Don't reveal everything at once. Slowly unveil clues and hints to keep readers guessing.

Use Sensory Details: Engage your reader's senses to create a more immersive experience.

Practice, Practice, Practice: The more you experiment with suspense, the better you'll become at using it effectively.

Remember: Suspense is a powerful tool that can transform your writing from ordinary to extraordinary. So, go forth and create stories that will leave your readers breathless!

I hope you enjoyed this lesson! Let me know if you have any questions or would like to explore this topic further.

ϷϷϷ

SIXTY-NINE

OFFER ALTERNATIVES—IT EMPOWERS OTHERS TO MAKE DECISIONS

The Art of Offering Alternatives: Empowering Others (and Yourself!)

Ever felt that nagging feeling of being "bossy" when you tell someone exactly what to do? Or maybe you've been on the receiving end of that, feeling like a puppet with someone else pulling the strings.

Well, let's ditch the dictatorship and embrace the power of choice! Today, we're diving deep into the art of offering alternatives – a skill that not only empowers others but also makes YOU a more effective and influential leader (or friend, or partner... you get the gist!).

Why Alternatives Rule the World

Think about it. When you're given a choice, you feel more invested in the outcome. You feel heard, respected, and like you have some control over your own destiny.

Imagine this: Your friend is struggling to choose a restaurant for dinner.

The "Bossy" Way: "Let's go to that new Italian place. I've been craving pasta."

The "Alternative" Way: "I'm feeling Italian tonight, but I'm also open to Mexican or maybe even that new Thai spot you were talking about."

See the difference? The second option gives your friend a sense of ownership. They feel like they're part of the decision-making process, making them more likely to be enthusiastic about the final choice.

👂👂👂

Ways to Influence (Without Being Influential!)

Now, let's get tactical. Here are a few sneaky ways to influence others while still giving them the power of choice:

The "Leading Question" Technique: "What are your thoughts on [option A] versus [option B]?" This subtly guides the conversation while letting them express their preferences.

The "Limited Options" Game: "We could go to the beach, or we could hike in the mountains. What sounds more appealing today?" (Notice how you're still presenting choices, even if they're limited.)

The "Benefit-Driven" Approach: "If we choose [option A], we'll get to [benefit A]. If we choose [option B], we'll have [benefit B]." This helps them weigh the pros and cons of each option.

👂👂👂

Let's Get Practical!

Ready to put your newfound knowledge to the test? Here are a couple of exercises:

The "Dinner Dilemma": Imagine you're planning a dinner party. Come up with at least three different appetizer options and present them to a friend, using the "Leading Question" technique.

The "Weekend Wonder": Plan a weekend getaway with a partner. Use the "Limited Options" game to narrow down your choices and involve them in the decision-making process.

Fun Fact:

Did you know that offering choices can actually increase cooperation and reduce conflict? It's true! People are more likely to buy into a plan if they feel like they had a say in it.

Humor Break: Remember that time you tried to "help" someone by making all the decisions for them? Yeah, let's all agree to never do that again.

Time for Reflection

How often do you find yourself making decisions for others without their input?

How does it feel when someone else makes all the decisions for you?

How can you start incorporating the art of offering alternatives into your daily interactions?

Actionable Insights

<u>Embrace the "Maybe" Mindset</u>: Instead of saying "no" outright, try "maybe, but..." or "that's an interesting idea, let's explore it further."

<u>Practice Active Listening</u>: Pay attention to what others are saying (and not saying) to truly understand their preferences.

<u>Celebrate Small Wins</u>: Acknowledge and appreciate the times when you successfully offer alternatives and empower others.

The Bottom Line

Offering alternatives is more than just being polite. It's about building stronger relationships, fostering collaboration, and creating a more positive and empowering environment for everyone involved. So, go forth and offer choices! The world will thank you for it.

Remember, there's no one-size-fits-all approach. The key is to find the balance between offering guidance and giving others the freedom to choose.

ᐅᐅᐅ

SEVENTY

END WITH A STRONG CALL TO ACTION—IT ENSURES FOLLOW-THROUGH

The Power of a Strong Call to Action

What is a Call to Action (CTA)?

A CTA is like a clear instruction or a nudge.

It tells people exactly what you want them to do next.

It could be something simple like "Learn More," or more specific like "Buy Now" or "Sign Up Today."

Why are CTAs important?

They guide people: Without a CTA, people might not know what to do after reading your message or seeing your content.

They increase engagement: A strong CTA encourages people to take the next step, whether it's visiting a website, making a purchase, or subscribing to a newsletter.

They help you achieve your goals: Whether you're trying to sell a product, raise awareness, or gather leads, a clear CTA helps you reach your desired outcome.

How to write a strong CTA:

Keep it short and sweet: Use concise and action-oriented language.

Be specific: Instead of "Learn More," try "Learn More About Our Free Trial."

Create a sense of urgency: Use words like "Limited Time Offer" or "Don't Miss Out."

Make it visually appealing: Use buttons, contrasting colors, and clear fonts to make your CTA stand out.

Test different CTAs: Experiment with different wording and placement to see what works best for your audience.

Examples of strong CTAs:

"Shop Now"

"Download Your Free Guide"

"Book Your Consultation Today"

"Join Our Community"

"Claim Your Discount"

Remember: A strong CTA is essential for any successful marketing campaign or communication. By clearly telling people what you want them to do, you increase the chances of them taking action and achieving your desired results.

Key takeaway: Always end your messages with a strong call to action to guide your audience and achieve your goals.

ᚦᚦᚦ

"Ways to Inspire" Focus on
motivating teams, public speaking,
and leadership communication

SEVENTY-ONE

LEAD BY EXAMPLE-YOUR ACTIONS COMMUNICATE LOUDER THAN WORDS

In life, words can be powerful, but actions carry far more weight. People are more likely to follow what you do than what you say. This is why the principle of "leading by example" is so important, whether you're a parent, teacher, manager, or leader in any role. Your actions set the tone for others and show them what is truly important.

Let's explore why leading by example is so effective and how you can incorporate it into your daily life.

The Power of Actions Over Words

Words are easy to say, but actions are harder to fake. For example, if a manager tells their team to work hard but constantly procrastinates, their words lose meaning. On the other hand, when leaders demonstrate dedication, punctuality, and responsibility, they inspire others to do the same.

Human beings learn by observing others. Psychologists call this "modeling," where people imitate the behavior they see in others, especially those they admire or respect. If you practice integrity, kindness, and perseverance, the people around you are more likely to adopt those values themselves.

ᗑᗑᗑ

Why Leading by Example Matters

Builds Trust

When your actions match your words, people trust you. They see that you are authentic and not just making empty promises. Trust is the foundation of strong relationships, whether in a family, workplace, or community.

Inspires Others

Actions inspire others more effectively than lectures or commands. If you work hard to achieve your goals, others will be motivated to follow your lead. Inspiration comes from showing people what is possible, not just telling them what to do.

Creates a Positive Culture

Leading by example creates a culture of accountability and respect. In a workplace, for instance, a leader who values teamwork and demonstrates it by collaborating with their team fosters a positive and productive environment.

Encourages Responsibility

When people see a leader taking responsibility for their actions, it encourages them to do the same. This eliminates the blame game and promotes accountability at all levels.

ppp

How to Lead by Example

Practice What You Preach

If you expect honesty, fairness, or discipline from others, make sure you embody those qualities. Your behavior should reflect the values you want to instill in others.

Be Consistent

Consistency builds credibility. For example, if you're a teacher who enforces punctuality, it's important to be punctual yourself. Inconsistency sends mixed messages and erodes trust.

Be Humble and Willing to Learn

Leaders who admit their mistakes and show a willingness to learn are highly respected. Humility shows that you're human and approachable, encouraging others to adopt the same mindset.

Stay Calm Under Pressure

How you handle challenges speaks volumes. If you remain calm and solution-focused in tough situations, others will follow suit. Emotional resilience is a key trait of effective leaders.

<u>Celebrate Efforts and Lead with Positivity</u>

Acknowledging the efforts of others and maintaining a positive attitude can have a ripple effect. Positivity inspires hope and determination, even in difficult times.

PPP

<u>Real-Life Examples of Leading by Example</u>

Parents: Children learn values like honesty, kindness, and respect by observing their parents. A parent who practices gratitude and patience sets a strong example for their children.

Workplace Leaders: A manager who works hard, listens to their team, and handles criticism gracefully creates a motivated and respectful work environment.

Community Leaders: Activists and community leaders who actively participate in solving local issues inspire others to contribute as well.

"Actions speak louder than words" isn't just a saying; it's a proven truth about how people learn and grow. By leading with your actions, you set a powerful example that words alone cannot achieve.

Whether you're guiding your children, motivating your team, or inspiring your community, remember that your behavior is a reflection of your values. Be the person you want others to become, and watch how your actions create positive change around you.

In the end, leading by example isn't just about influencing others—it's about becoming the best version of yourself. And when you do that, you naturally encourage others to do the same.

What actions will you take today to lead by example?

PPP

SEVENTY-TWO

USE INSPIRATIONAL QUOTES TO UPLIFT CONVERSATIONS

Words have the power to inspire, motivate, and connect us. Sometimes, a single phrase can spark a meaningful conversation or uplift someone's spirit. Inspirational quotes are like little treasures of wisdom—simple yet impactful. They can turn a mundane conversation into something memorable and empowering.

In this article, let's explore how you can use inspirational quotes to enhance your conversations, strengthen relationships, and spread positivity.

Why Inspirational Quotes Matter in Conversations

<u>They Spark Positivity</u>

Quotes often carry a positive message, which can shift the tone of a conversation. Whether it's encouraging someone going through a tough time or celebrating a small success, sharing an uplifting quote can create a moment of joy and hope.

<u>They Connect People</u>

Sharing a quote that resonates with both you and the other person creates a deeper bond. It shows that you've thought about their feelings or situation and that you care enough to offer meaningful words.

<u>They Encourage Reflection</u>

A well-timed quote can make someone stop and think. It may offer a new perspective or encourage them to reflect on their goals, challenges, or values.

<u>They Make Conversations Memorable</u>

Adding an inspiring quote to your conversation can leave a lasting impression. People often remember the quotes and the person who shared them, making your words stand out.

ϸϸϸ

When to Use Inspirational Quotes in Conversations

<u>To Offer Support</u>

If someone is feeling low or overwhelmed, sharing a quote like "This too shall pass" or "Every storm runs out of rain" can bring comfort. It shows empathy and reminds them that challenges are temporary.

<u>To Celebrate Achievements</u>

When someone accomplishes something, big or small, an inspiring quote can amplify the celebration. For example, "The journey of a thousand miles begins with a single step" is perfect for someone starting a new adventure.

<u>To Motivate Action</u>

If a friend or colleague is hesitant to take the next step, a motivational quote can give them the push they need. Quotes like "Believe you can, and you're halfway there" can ignite their confidence.

<u>To Start a Meaningful Discussion</u>

A powerful quote can act as a conversation starter. For example, asking someone their thoughts on "Happiness is not something ready-made. It comes from your own actions" can lead to a deep and enriching dialogue.

<u>To Share Wisdom</u>

Sometimes, sharing a quote in a casual chat can offer wisdom without sounding preachy. For instance, "Be the change you wish to see in the world" is a gentle way to inspire someone to take positive actions.

ϸϸϸ

How to Use Inspirational Quotes Effectively

<u>Choose Quotes That Fit the Moment</u>

Select quotes that are relevant to the conversation or the person's situation. A meaningful quote is more impactful when it resonates with the context.

<u>Keep It Simple</u>

Avoid using long or overly complex quotes. Short and simple quotes are easier to understand and remember. For example, "Success is not final, failure is not fatal" is a concise and effective quote for encouraging resilience.

<u>Deliver with Sincerity</u>

When you share a quote, make sure it feels genuine. Your tone and intention matter. Speak from the heart, and the person will feel the sincerity behind your words.

Explain Why the Quote Resonates with You

To make your quote more relatable, share a brief personal story or explain why it's meaningful to you. For example, "This quote helped me during a difficult time, and I thought it might help you too."

<u>Don't Overdo It</u>

While quotes are powerful, using them too often in a single conversation can dilute their impact. Use them sparingly to maintain their effectiveness.

Examples of Inspirational Quotes to Uplift Conversations

Here are a few timeless quotes you can use:

For Encouragement:

"It always seems impossible until it's done." – Nelson Mandela

For Positivity:

"Keep your face always toward the sunshine, and shadows will fall behind you." – Walt Whitman

For Resilience:

"Fall seven times, stand up eight." – Japanese Proverb

For Self-Belief:

"You are braver than you believe, stronger than you seem, and smarter than you think." – A.A. Milne

For Taking Action:

"The best way to predict the future is to create it." – Peter Drucker

ppp

The Impact of Inspirational Quotes

When used thoughtfully, inspirational quotes can create a ripple effect of positivity. They can brighten someone's day, shift their mindset, or even help them make an important decision. Conversations infused with uplifting quotes often leave people feeling seen, heard, and valued.

In a world that sometimes feels overwhelming, small acts of kindness—like sharing an inspirational quote—can make a big difference. Quotes carry the wisdom of great thinkers, poets, and leaders. By passing them along, you're not just sharing words; you're sharing hope, encouragement, and positivity.

The next time you're in a conversation, think of how you can use a quote to uplift someone. After all, the right words at the right time can leave a lasting impact. So, go ahead and let your conversations inspire and empower others!

❦❦❦

SEVENTY-THREE

IT'S RELATABLE- SHARE PERSONAL CHALLENGES AND HOW YOU OVERCAME THEM

Everyone has faced challenges in life, whether big or small. These struggles shape who we are and help us grow stronger. Sharing your personal challenges and how you overcame them can inspire others, build deeper connections, and create a sense of community. When we open up about our experiences, we show others that they are not alone, and we provide hope that challenges can be overcome.

Let's explore why sharing personal challenges is powerful, how to share them effectively, and the positive impact it can have on others and yourself.

Why Sharing Personal Challenges Matters

It Creates Connection

When you share your struggles, others can relate to you on a human level. It helps people see that they're not the only ones facing difficulties and builds empathy between you and the listener.

It Inspires and Motivates

Sharing how you overcame a tough situation can inspire others to face their own challenges. Your story can become a source of motivation and hope for someone who may be feeling lost or discouraged.

<u>It Breaks the Stigma Around Struggles</u>

Many people feel ashamed of their problems, thinking they are the only ones going through them. By sharing your experiences, you help break the stigma and normalize the fact that everyone faces difficulties at some point.

<u>It Promotes Personal Growth</u>

Talking about your challenges helps you reflect on how far you've come. It reminds you of your inner strength and resilience, boosting your confidence.

ppp

How to Share Your Personal Challenges Effectively

<u>Be Honest and Genuine</u>

Authenticity is key. Don't sugarcoat your experience or pretend it was easier than it really was. People connect with honesty, and sharing your real emotions will make your story more relatable.

<u>Focus on the Lessons Learned</u>

While it's important to talk about the challenge, the real value comes from sharing what you learned and how you grew from the experience. Highlight the steps you took to overcome the situation and the wisdom you gained along the way.

<u>Adapt to Your Audience</u>

Consider who you're sharing your story with. If you're talking to friends, you might share more personal details, while in a professional setting, you could focus on challenges related to work or career growth.

<u>Keep a Positive Tone</u>

Even if your story involves hardship, end on a hopeful note. Show how you found strength and overcame the odds. A positive ending will leave your audience feeling uplifted.

<u>Don't Overshare</u>

While being open is important, avoid going into unnecessary details that might make others uncomfortable. Share enough to make your story impactful, but keep it balanced.

ppp

Examples of Personal Challenges to Share

Here are some common challenges that many people can relate to, along with ways to talk about them:

Overcoming Fear or Doubt

Share a time when self-doubt held you back and how you learned to believe in yourself. For example:

"I used to be terrified of public speaking, but I joined a local group to practice. Over time, I built my confidence and can now speak in front of large audiences without fear."

Recovering from Failure

Talk about a failure you experienced and how you bounced back. For example:

"I once started a business that didn't work out. At first, I felt defeated, but I used the lessons I learned to start a second business, which became successful."

Dealing with a Personal Loss

Share how you coped with losing someone important to you and found healing. For example:

"When I lost my best friend, it felt like my world had ended. But I found comfort in journaling, talking to others, and focusing on the good memories we shared."

Navigating Career Challenges

Share how you overcame obstacles in your career. For example:

"I was once passed over for a promotion, and it felt like a huge setback. But instead of giving up, I worked on improving my skills and eventually earned a leadership role."

Improving Mental or Physical Health

Talk about how you faced and overcame a health challenge. For example:

"I struggled with anxiety for years, but through therapy and mindfulness practices, I've learned how to manage it and feel more at peace."

The Positive Impact of Sharing Your Story

<u>Empowering Others</u>

Your story might be exactly what someone needs to hear. It can encourage them to take the first step toward solving their own problems.

<u>Fostering Understanding</u>

When you share your experiences, you help others see things from a different perspective. This fosters compassion and understanding in your community.

<u>Building Stronger Relationships</u>

Sharing personal challenges builds trust and strengthens your relationships. It shows vulnerability, which makes people feel closer to you.

<u>Boosting Your Confidence</u>

Recognizing and sharing how you've overcome difficulties reminds you of your resilience. It's a powerful reminder of your ability to face future challenges.

Life is full of ups and downs, but it's the challenges that shape us into stronger, wiser, and more compassionate people. By sharing your personal challenges and how you overcame them, you can inspire others, build connections, and create a positive ripple effect in the world.

Remember, you don't need to have a perfect story. The simple act of opening up and being vulnerable is enough to make an impact. So, the next time you're in a conversation, don't hesitate to share your journey. Your story might be the light someone else needs to guide their way.

What challenge have you overcome that you'd like to share with others?

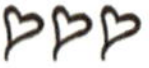

SEVENTY-FOUR

ACKNOWLEDGE AND CELEBRATE OTHERS' CONTRIBUTIONS

We all want to feel valued and appreciated for the work we do. Whether it's at home, in the workplace, or within a community, acknowledging and celebrating others' contributions is a simple yet powerful way to build stronger relationships, foster teamwork, and boost morale.

When we take the time to recognize the efforts of those around us, we create an environment where people feel motivated, respected, and inspired to do their best. In this article, let's explore why acknowledging others' contributions is important, how to do it effectively, and the positive impact it creates for everyone involved.

Why Acknowledging Others' Contributions Matters

It Builds Confidence

Recognition boosts confidence and self-esteem. When people know their efforts are noticed, they feel valued and are more likely to take on challenges with enthusiasm.

It Strengthens Relationships

Acknowledging someone's hard work shows that you appreciate and respect them. This strengthens trust and fosters better communication, whether in personal relationships or professional settings.

It Encourages Teamwork

In group settings, celebrating contributions promotes a sense of unity. It reminds everyone that their efforts are essential to achieving shared goals.

<u>It Creates a Positive Environment</u>

Recognition contributes to a positive atmosphere, where people feel happy and motivated. A little appreciation goes a long way in reducing stress and improving overall well-being.

ϷϷϷ

Ways to Acknowledge and Celebrate Others' Contributions

<u>Give Verbal Appreciation</u>

A simple "thank you" or "great job" can brighten someone's day. Be specific about what you're praising to make your recognition more meaningful. For example:

"Thank you for staying late to finish the report. Your hard work really helped us meet the deadline."

<u>Write a Note of Gratitude</u>

A handwritten note or even a thoughtful email can make a big impact. Taking the time to write your appreciation shows that you truly value their efforts.

<u>Celebrate Publicly</u>

Recognize someone's achievements in front of others, such as during a team meeting, family gathering, or community event. Public recognition can be incredibly uplifting and sets an example for others to follow.

<u>Offer Small Rewards</u>

Rewards don't have to be grand or expensive. A small gift, a coffee treat, or even a shoutout on social media can go a long way in showing your appreciation.

<u>Highlight Their Strengths</u>

Point out the unique skills or qualities that someone brings to the table. For example:

"Your creativity and attention to detail really brought this project to life. We couldn't have done it without you!"

<u>Celebrate Milestones</u>

Acknowledge not just big achievements but also smaller milestones along the way. For instance, celebrating a team member's first successful project or a student's consistent effort can be incredibly motivating.

<u>Listen and Show Interest</u>

Sometimes, simply listening to someone and showing interest in their work or ideas can be a powerful way to acknowledge their contributions.

ϷϷϷ

The Ripple Effect of Recognition

<u>Increased Motivation</u>

When people feel appreciated, they are more motivated to work hard and contribute further. Recognition energizes individuals and inspires them to give their best.

<u>Improved Morale</u>

Celebrating contributions creates a culture of positivity, where people feel happy and proud of their work. High morale leads to better productivity and satisfaction.

<u>Encourages Others to Contribute</u>

Acknowledging one person's effort often inspires others to step up and contribute. Recognition sets a standard for teamwork and encourages everyone to work together.

<u>Builds a Supportive Culture</u>

In workplaces, schools, or communities, a culture of recognition fosters collaboration and support. People feel they are part of something meaningful, which strengthens bonds and loyalty.

ᐅᐅᐅ

Practical Examples of Acknowledging Contributions

<u>In the Workplace</u>:

Recognize a colleague's extra effort during a busy season. For example: "Your dedication to this project made all the difference. Thank you for going above and beyond!"

Celebrate team successes with a small event or a thank-you lunch.

In Personal Relationships:

Appreciate your partner's efforts in daily life. For instance: "Thank you for making dinner tonight. It means a lot to me after a long day."

Acknowledge a friend's support by saying, "I really appreciate you being there for me when I needed help."

In Community Settings:

Highlight the efforts of volunteers in community projects. For example: "Thank you to everyone who came together to organize this event. Your hard work made it a success!"

Nominate someone for a community award or recognition.

Acknowledging and celebrating others' contributions is more than just good manners—it's a powerful way to uplift and inspire those around you.

It creates an environment where people feel valued, motivated, and connected.

Remember, recognition doesn't always have to be big or elaborate. Even small gestures of appreciation can make a big difference. Whether it's a kind word, a note of thanks, or a simple acknowledgment in a group setting, your effort to recognize someone's contributions can have a lasting positive impact.

So, take a moment today to appreciate the people around you. Celebrate their hard work, acknowledge their strengths, and let them know how much they mean to you. After all, a little recognition goes a long way in making the world a better and more supportive place.

ᗧᗧᗧ

SEVENTY-FIVE

PAINT A VIVID VISION OF SUCCESS FOR YOUR AUDIENCE

Success is a powerful motivator, but it means different things to different people. Whether you're a leader, a teacher, or a content creator, your ability to inspire others depends on how clearly you can describe what success looks like. When you paint a vivid picture of success, you give your audience something to strive for—an exciting destination that feels tangible and within reach.

In this article, we'll explore why it's important to share a clear vision of success, how to craft a compelling picture of the future, and the impact it can have on motivating and guiding your audience.

Why a Clear Vision of Success Matters

It Creates Purpose

A clear vision gives people something to aim for. It helps them understand why their efforts matter and how their actions contribute to the bigger picture.

It Inspires Motivation

When people can vividly imagine the rewards of their hard work, they feel more excited and energized to pursue their goals. A vision of success acts as a source of motivation, especially during challenging times.

It Builds Focus

A detailed vision provides direction. It keeps your audience focused on what truly matters and helps them avoid distractions.

<u>It Encourages Commitment</u>
When people see a bright future ahead, they're more likely to commit to the journey. A shared vision unites everyone around a common goal.

ϷϷϷ

How to Paint a Vivid Vision of Success
<u>Be Specific and Descriptive</u>
Don't just say, "Success is achieving greatness." Instead, describe it in vivid detail. For example:
"Imagine a workplace where everyone feels valued, creative ideas flow freely, and we celebrate big wins together as a team."
Specific details make the vision feel real and relatable.
<u>Use Positive and Exciting Language</u>
The words you choose matter. Use language that excites and uplifts your audience. For example, instead of saying, "It will be hard, but we'll make it," say, "The path may be challenging, but every step will bring us closer to something amazing!"
<u>Include Sensory Details</u>
Appeal to the senses to make your vision come alive. For instance:
"Picture yourself standing on stage, feeling the warmth of the spotlight as the audience applauds your achievement. The joy and pride in that moment are unforgettable."
Sensory details help people imagine themselves in the vision.
<u>Show the Benefits</u>
Explain how success will improve their lives. Will it bring happiness, growth, or new opportunities? For example:
"When we complete this project, we'll not only achieve our goals but also prove to ourselves that we're capable of anything we set our minds to."
<u>Make It Personal</u>
Tailor your vision to your audience's needs and aspirations. Use examples that resonate with their experiences and values.
<u>Show the Journey, Not Just the Destination</u>
While the end goal is important, also describe the process of getting there. For example:
"Success isn't just about the finish line. It's about the lessons we'll learn, the friendships we'll build, and the growth we'll experience along the way."

ϷϷϷ

Examples of Vivid Visions of Success

<u>For a Team</u>

"Imagine walking into an office where everyone is excited to be here. Collaboration is at its peak, ideas are turning into breakthroughs, and our hard work is being recognized by people around the world. Together, we're building a future we can all be proud of."

<u>For Students</u>

"Picture yourself standing on graduation day, holding your diploma with a smile that says, 'I did it.' The struggles, the sleepless nights, and the challenges will all be worth it as you step confidently into the next chapter of your life."

<u>For a Community</u>

"Visualize a neighborhood where families come together, children play safely in the parks, and everyone works toward a common goal. Together, we can create a thriving, supportive community where everyone feels they belong."

ᗽᗽᗽ

The Impact of a Vivid Vision of Success

It Unites People

A shared vision brings people together. It fosters teamwork and collaboration because everyone is working toward the same dream.

It Sparks Action

When people see a clear and exciting future, they're more likely to take action. A vivid vision turns "someday" into "let's start today."

It Builds Confidence

A compelling vision reminds people of their potential and encourages them to believe in their ability to succeed.

It Keeps People Going

During tough times, a vision of success acts as a beacon of hope. It reminds people why they started and keeps them moving forward.

A vivid vision of success is like a roadmap—it shows the way forward and makes the destination feel real. By describing success in clear, exciting terms, you inspire your audience to believe in the possibilities and work toward their goals with confidence and determination.

As a leader, teacher, or influencer, you have the power to shape how others see the future. So, take the time to craft a vision that speaks to their hearts and minds. Use vivid details, uplifting language, and relatable examples to make your vision come alive.

Remember, when people can clearly see what's possible, they'll feel inspired to make it a reality. What vision of success will you share with your audience today?

❧❧❧

SEVENTY-SIX

SPEAK WITH PASSION-IT'S CONTAGIOUS

Passion is a powerful force. When you speak with passion, your energy, enthusiasm, and excitement naturally draw people in. Whether you're giving a presentation, telling a story, or sharing your ideas, passion has the ability to inspire, motivate, and connect with others on a deeper level.

When people hear someone speak passionately, they feel it. It's contagious—it can light up a room and ignite interest and excitement in the hearts of the audience. In this article, we'll explore why speaking with passion is so impactful, how to channel your passion effectively, and how it can positively influence those around you.

Why Speaking with Passion Matters

It Grabs Attention

Passionate speakers stand out. Their enthusiasm captures the audience's attention, making people want to listen. When your voice carries energy and emotion, people naturally lean in to hear what you have to say.

It Makes Your Message Memorable

Passion brings life to your words. When you speak with excitement and conviction, your message becomes more impactful and memorable. People may forget facts, but they'll remember how you made them feel.

It Inspires Action

Passionate speech doesn't just inform—it motivates. It can move people to take action, make changes, or pursue their own goals with newfound energy.

It Builds Connection

When you speak with passion, you share a part of yourself. Your authenticity and excitement resonate with others, creating a sense of trust and connection.

ﭖﭖﭖ

How to Speak with Passion

Know Your Topic Inside and Out

Passion comes naturally when you care deeply about your topic. Take the time to learn and understand what you're speaking about. The more confident you are in your knowledge, the more passionate and convincing you'll sound.

Find Your "Why"

Ask yourself, "Why does this matter to me?" Understanding the personal significance of your message will help you speak with genuine emotion. For example, if you're talking about environmental conservation, think about how nature has personally impacted your life.

Use Your Voice Effectively

Your tone, pace, and volume can convey passion just as much as your words.

Vary your tone: Use highs and lows in your voice to emphasize key points.

Pause for impact: Pauses create drama and allow your audience to process your message.

Speak with energy: Avoid monotone delivery—let your excitement shine through.

Show Emotion

Don't be afraid to let your emotions show. Whether it's joy, determination, or even vulnerability, sharing your feelings helps your audience connect with you on a human level.

Use Body Language

Your body speaks, too. Use gestures, facial expressions, and movement to amplify your passion. For instance, a smile, a confident posture, or a hand movement can make your message more dynamic and engaging.

Engage Your Audience

Interact with your audience by asking questions, sharing relatable stories, or encouraging participation. When people feel involved, they're more likely to catch your passion.

Practice and Prepare

Even the most passionate speakers need preparation. Practice your delivery to ensure your passion comes across naturally and confidently. Rehearsing will also help you avoid distractions or nervousness.

ᗉᗉᗉ

The Impact of Passionate Speaking

<u>Inspiration Spreads</u>

When you speak passionately, you inspire others to care about your message. Your energy becomes infectious, encouraging others to feel excited or motivated about the topic.

<u>Confidence Grows</u>

Speaking with passion boosts your confidence. The more you believe in what you're saying, the more powerful and self-assured you'll feel. This confidence also reassures your audience that your message is worth listening to.

<u>People Remember You</u>

Passion makes you unforgettable. Whether you're speaking at a meeting, giving a speech, or having a one-on-one conversation, your passion leaves a lasting impression.

<u>It Fosters Change</u>

Passionate speeches have the power to change minds and hearts. From leaders to activists, the most influential people in history often moved others through their passionate words.

ᗉᗉᗉ

Real-Life Examples of Passionate Speaking

Martin Luther King Jr.'s "I Have a Dream" Speech

Dr. King's famous speech is a timeless example of passionate speaking. His heartfelt delivery, powerful voice, and emotional connection inspired millions and continues to move people today.

A Teacher Encouraging Students

A passionate teacher who believes in their students can spark curiosity and confidence in the classroom. For example: "I know you can do this. You have the potential to achieve great things, and I'm here to support you every step of the way!"

A Leader Motivating Their Team

A manager who speaks with passion about their vision can unite their team. For instance: "Together, we can create something incredible. Every one of you plays an important role, and I believe in what we can achieve as a team."

Passion is a gift you can share through your words. When you speak with passion, you don't just communicate information—you inspire feelings, ignite enthusiasm, and create connections.

To speak with passion, you don't have to be perfect. You simply need to care deeply about what you're saying and express it with genuine energy. Your passion will naturally draw others in and leave a lasting impact.

So, the next time you speak, let your passion shine. Whether you're delivering a speech, motivating a team, or simply having a conversation, speak with excitement, confidence, and heart. Your energy is contagious, and your words can inspire others to see the world in a whole new way.

ppp

SEVENTY-SEVEN
USE HUMOR- IT BREAKS BARRIERS AND CREATES A POSITIVE ATMOSPHERE

Humor is a powerful tool in communication. It has the incredible ability to break down walls, connect people, and create a positive atmosphere. In both personal and professional settings, humor can make a big difference. Whether you're leading a team, conducting a presentation, or just having a casual conversation, humor can help people feel more comfortable, engage better, and build stronger relationships.

Why is Humor Important?

It Breaks the Ice: One of the first things that humor can do is break the ice. In any new situation, whether it's a job interview, meeting new clients, or attending a conference, people tend to feel a little awkward. Humor can lighten the mood, make people laugh, and suddenly, the tension melts away. When the environment feels less serious, everyone feels more at ease.

It Builds Connection: Humor creates common ground. A good laugh is something everyone can share. When you make people laugh, you invite them to connect with you on a personal level. This is especially useful in leadership and team-building activities. When leaders use humor, they seem more approachable, which builds trust and stronger relationships. In fact, studies show that teams with leaders who can laugh and share light moments together are often more productive.

It Eases Tension: Sometimes, work can get stressful. Deadlines, challenges, and conflicts can create a tense atmosphere. Humor acts as a reset button. A well-timed joke or funny comment can break the tension, redirect people's focus, and restore balance. In high-stress situations, humor helps everyone relax and refocus on the task at hand.

It Encourages Creativity: Humor opens the mind. When we laugh, our brains release endorphins, which improve mood and promote creative thinking. In brainstorming sessions or problem-solving discussions, introducing humor can spark new ideas and encourage innovative thinking. Humor challenges conventional thinking, and as a result, creativity flourishes.

It Makes You Memorable: People tend to remember those who make them laugh. Humor has the power to make you stand out in people's minds, whether it's in a presentation, a meeting, or even on social media. Being memorable is a huge asset in the business world, where networking and building relationships are key. When people enjoy being around you because of your humor, they are more likely to remember you and your ideas.

ᛈᛈᛈ

How to Use Humor Effectively

Know Your Audience: The type of humor you use should depend on your audience. What makes a team of professionals laugh may differ from what a group of friends finds funny. Always consider the context and the people you're addressing. The best humor is relevant, respectful, and inclusive.

Be Yourself: Authenticity matters. Don't force humor that doesn't feel natural to you. If you're not someone who regularly tells jokes, you don't have to suddenly become a comedian. Simple, light-hearted comments can have a big impact. Sometimes, self-deprecating humor (joking about yourself in a light way) can be especially effective because it shows humility and relatability.

Avoid Offending: While humor can bring people together, it's important to steer clear of humor that may offend. Jokes about sensitive topics or anything that might alienate others should be avoided. The goal is to create a positive atmosphere, not to make someone uncomfortable.

Timing is Everything: Humor is all about timing. A well-timed joke or light-hearted comment can change the energy in a room instantly. On the other hand, using humor at the wrong moment (like during a serious conversation or a tense situation) can have the opposite effect. Learn when humor fits into the conversation and when it's best to hold back.

Humor is more than just a way to make people laugh – it's a tool that fosters connection, reduces tension, and creates a positive environment. Whether in the workplace, in social situations, or in public speaking, humor can help break barriers and bring people closer together.

By using humor effectively, you not only brighten someone's day but also open doors for better communication and stronger relationships. So, next time you face a challenging situation, don't forget to add a little humor – it could be the key to success!

ᐅᐅᐅ

SEVENTY-EIGHT

GIVE CONSTRUCTIVE FEEDBACK WITH A POSITIVE TONE

Providing feedback is one of the most powerful tools for growth, both for individuals and teams. However, feedback can sometimes feel daunting—especially when you need to address areas for improvement. The key is delivering it in a way that is not only helpful but also motivating. Constructive feedback, when given with a positive tone, can encourage development, foster improvement, and maintain strong relationships.

Why is Constructive Feedback Important?

<u>Promotes Growth and Development</u>: Constructive feedback helps individuals understand their strengths and areas for improvement. When communicated properly, feedback is a guide to help them grow and get better at what they do. Without feedback, there is no clear direction on how to improve, which can lead to stagnation.

<u>Builds Trust and Respect</u>: Providing feedback in a positive, respectful manner shows that you care about the person's success. When people feel valued and supported, they are more likely to trust you, accept your feedback, and take action. This creates an environment where continuous improvement thrives.

<u>Boosts Motivation</u>: Positive feedback motivates people to keep going. When delivered in a constructive way, it doesn't just focus on the mistakes, but also highlights the areas where they did well. This balance can uplift someone's spirits and encourage them to strive for better performance

without feeling discouraged.

ррр

How to Give Constructive Feedback with a Positive Tone

Start with the Positive: Always begin by acknowledging what the person has done well. This sets a positive tone for the conversation. When you start with praise, it shows that you notice their efforts and accomplishments. This makes them more receptive to the feedback that follows.

Example: "I really appreciate how you handled the customer inquiry today. You were very patient and clear in your explanation."

Be Specific and Focused: Avoid vague statements like "Do better next time." Instead, focus on specific actions or behaviors that can be improved. Offering examples helps the person understand what exactly needs to change. This clarity prevents confusion and gives them a clear direction.

Example: "In this case, I noticed that when you were responding to the inquiry, it took a bit longer to address the main issue. Maybe focusing on the key concern first would speed things up."

Offer Solutions, Not Just Criticism: Constructive feedback should come with suggestions on how to improve. Offering solutions helps the person understand what steps they can take to enhance their performance. This turns the feedback into a learning opportunity.

Example: "Maybe you could try practicing prioritizing the customer's main concern at the beginning of the conversation. It could help you address the issue more quickly and create a better experience for the customer."

Use "I" Statements Instead of "You" Statements: Using "I" statements makes the feedback less confrontational. It expresses that you are sharing your perspective and are offering support, not placing blame. This way, the feedback doesn't sound like an accusation.

Example: "I noticed the report had a few formatting issues. I believe that paying closer attention to the style guide can help ensure everything is consistent."

vs.

"You always make mistakes in the report format."

Encourage and Motivate: End the feedback by showing confidence in the person's ability to improve. Let them know that you believe in their potential and that you are there to support them through the process. This makes the feedback feel like a collaborative effort rather than a one-sided critique.

Example: "You've made great progress so far, and I'm confident that with a little more practice, you'll get even better. I'm here to support you along the way."

Create an Open Dialogue: Encourage the person to ask questions or share their perspective. Feedback should be a two-way conversation, not just a one-way critique. Creating an open dialogue fosters trust and ensures that the feedback is understood and well-received.

Example: "Do you have any thoughts on how you can improve this, or is there anything you need help with?"

ᗄᗄᗄ

The Balance Between Positive and Constructive Feedback

It's important to strike a balance between positive and constructive feedback. Too much positivity without direction can leave people unsure of what to improve, while too much criticism can demotivate and discourage. The key is to ensure the feedback is balanced, offering both recognition of strengths and clear, actionable steps for improvement.

Giving constructive feedback with a positive tone is a skill that can make a world of difference in how feedback is received and acted upon. By starting with praise, being specific, offering solutions, and maintaining a supportive tone, you can create an environment of growth, trust, and motivation.

Remember, feedback is not about pointing out flaws; it's about guiding others toward success. So, the next time you provide feedback, do it in a way that uplifts and empowers.

ᗄᗄᗄ

SEVENTY-NINE
ADAPT YOUR COMMUNICATION STYLE TO SUIT THE AUDIENCE

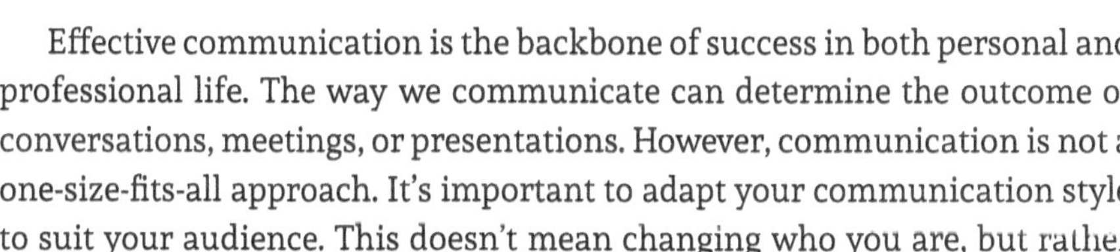

Effective communication is the backbone of success in both personal and professional life. The way we communicate can determine the outcome of conversations, meetings, or presentations. However, communication is not a one-size-fits-all approach. It's important to adapt your communication style to suit your audience. This doesn't mean changing who you are, but rather adjusting the way you present your message depending on the people you're speaking to.

Why is Adapting Your Communication Style Important?

<u>Ensures Clear Understanding</u>: Different people have different levels of understanding and ways of processing information. Adapting your communication style helps ensure your message is received and understood in the way you intend. Whether you're speaking to a colleague, a client, or a group of students, adapting ensures that your message doesn't get lost in translation.

<u>Builds Stronger Connections</u>: When you adapt your communication, it shows that you understand and respect your audience's needs. Whether they are introverts or extroverts, technical experts or beginners, adjusting your style makes them feel heard and valued. This builds rapport and trust, which is essential for strong relationships.

<u>Fosters Better Engagement</u>: A communication style that suits your audience keeps them engaged. When people feel comfortable with the way you're speaking, they are more likely to participate in discussions, ask questions, and offer feedback. On the other hand, when the style doesn't fit, people might zone out or become disengaged.

<u>Improves Influence and Persuasion</u>: If you want to persuade or influence others, it's crucial to communicate in a way that resonates with them. Adapting your communication style helps you present your arguments in a manner that appeals to their interests, needs, and understanding. This increases the likelihood of getting the response you want.

ᗄᗄᗄ

How to Adapt Your Communication Style to Suit the Audience

<u>Know Your Audience</u>: The first step in adapting your communication style is understanding your audience. Who are you speaking to? Are they technical experts, beginners, or laypeople? Are they formal or informal? What are their interests and concerns? The more you know about your audience, the better you can tailor your message. For instance, if you're speaking to a group of engineers, you may use more technical terms, while with a non-technical audience, you might simplify your language.

<u>Adjust Your Tone</u>: The tone of your message plays a significant role in how it is received. A formal tone might be appropriate for a business meeting or a professional presentation, while a casual tone works better in social settings or when speaking to friends and colleagues. Understanding the level of formality required helps you avoid sounding too stiff or too informal for the situation.

<u>Use the Right Language</u>: The language you choose should align with your audience's familiarity with the topic. If you're explaining a complex process to beginners, use simple and clear language. Avoid jargon or technical terms unless your audience is familiar with them. On the other hand, if you're speaking to a specialized group, using industry-specific terms may be more appropriate. The goal is to make sure your audience understands and follows your message easily.

<u>Adapt Your Body Language</u>: Communication isn't just about words—it's also about non-verbal cues. Your body language, facial expressions, and gestures play a vital role in how your message is perceived. In formal settings, it's essential to maintain good posture and make eye contact. In informal settings, you can be more relaxed with your body language, but

still, maintain an open and approachable demeanor. Adapting your body language shows that you are in tune with your audience and the situation.

Consider the Medium: The way you communicate can vary depending on the medium—whether it's a face-to-face meeting, email, phone call, or video conference. When communicating through email, for example, you may need to be more direct and concise, as it's a more written form of communication. In a face-to-face meeting, you have the opportunity to use gestures and intonation to emphasize key points. Each medium requires a different communication approach, so adjust accordingly.

Be an Active Listener: To communicate effectively, it's important to listen as much as you speak. Pay attention to your audience's reactions, both verbal and non-verbal. If they seem confused or disengaged, adjust your approach on the spot. If they seem excited or curious, you may want to delve deeper into the topic. Active listening helps you gauge how your message is being received and allows you to adapt in real-time.

Examples of Adapting Communication Styles:

In a Team Meeting: If you're leading a team meeting with colleagues, you might use a collaborative and inclusive style. You can ask open-ended questions, encourage participation, and keep the tone light. This approach makes everyone feel comfortable and valued. However, in a one-on-one meeting with a senior manager, your tone would be more formal and focused, ensuring that the communication remains professional and respectful.

Presenting to Clients: When presenting to clients, it's essential to adjust your communication to their level of understanding and interest. A technical client may appreciate a deep dive into data and specifics, while a non-technical client may appreciate a more straightforward, solution-oriented presentation. The key is to adjust the depth of information and the language used according to their needs.

Teaching or Training: If you're training a group of new hires, use simple explanations, visuals, and examples that relate to their daily tasks. If you're speaking to seasoned professionals, you might present more advanced concepts and encourage more discussion and problem-solving.

Adapting your communication style to suit your audience is not about changing who you are but about being flexible enough to connect in ways that work for others. It ensures your message is understood, encourages engagement, and builds stronger relationships.

Whether you're speaking to a team, clients, or a large audience, tailoring your approach based on their needs, preferences, and understanding makes all the difference.

So, the next time you communicate, take a moment to consider who you are speaking to and adjust your style accordingly. It's a small change that can lead to significant results!

ᗡᗡᗡ

• 235 •

EIGHTY

CULTIVATE A CULTURE OF GROWTH- IT DRIVES RESULTS

In today's rapidly changing world, businesses that stand still are destined to fall behind. To thrive, organizations need to foster a culture of continuous growth and improvement. This isn't just about boosting profits; it's about creating an environment where employees are empowered, innovative, and passionate about their work.

What is a Growth Culture?

A growth culture is more than just buzzwords. It's a mindset that permeates every level of the organization.

It's about:

<u>Embracing Challenges</u>: Viewing setbacks as opportunities to learn and grow.

<u>Continuous Learning</u>: Encouraging employees to constantly acquire new skills and knowledge.

<u>Open Communication</u>: Fostering a transparent and honest environment where feedback is valued and acted upon.

<u>Innovation</u>: Supporting and rewarding creative ideas and experimentation.

<u>Employee Empowerment</u>: Giving employees the autonomy and resources to make decisions and take ownership of their work.

<u>Recognition and Rewards</u>: Acknowledging and celebrating individual and team achievements.

ᗏᗏᗏ

Why is a Growth Culture Important?

A strong growth culture brings numerous benefits:

Increased Employee Engagement: When employees feel valued and empowered, they are more likely to be engaged and motivated.

Improved Innovation: A culture that encourages experimentation and risk-taking leads to more creative solutions and new products/services.

Enhanced Productivity: When employees are constantly learning and improving, they become more efficient and effective in their roles.

Stronger Employer Brand: A company known for its growth culture attracts top talent, making it easier to recruit and retain skilled employees.

Competitive Advantage: In a dynamic market, a growth mindset is crucial for staying ahead of the competition.

ᗏᗏᗏ

How to Cultivate a Growth Culture

Building a growth culture requires a multi-faceted approach:

Lead by Example: Leaders must demonstrate a commitment to growth and continuous improvement.

Invest in Employee Development: Provide opportunities for training, mentorship, and professional development.

Create a Supportive Environment: Encourage open communication, feedback, and collaboration.

Celebrate Successes: Recognize and reward individual and team achievements.

Encourage Risk-Taking: Create a safe space for employees to experiment and try new things.

Gather Employee Feedback: Regularly solicit and act on employee feedback to identify areas for improvement.

Cultivating a culture of growth is an ongoing journey, not a destination. It requires consistent effort and a commitment to continuous improvement.

By prioritizing employee development, fostering innovation, and creating a supportive environment, organizations can unlock their full potential and achieve sustainable success.

ᗏᗏᗏ

EIGHTY-ONE

SHARE SUCCESS STORIES FROM OTHERS—IT MOTIVATES AND BUILDS BELIEF

We all need a little inspiration now and then. Whether it's facing a challenging project, overcoming a personal obstacle, or simply navigating the ups and downs of daily life, hearing about others' triumphs can be incredibly motivating.

The Power of Success Stories

Success stories have a unique ability to:

Inspire Action: When we hear about someone else overcoming a similar challenge, it gives us the belief that we can do it too. It sparks a sense of possibility and encourages us to take action towards our own goals.

Build Confidence: Hearing about others' successes can help us overcome self-doubt and build our own self-belief. We realize that our dreams are attainable and that we have the potential to achieve great things.

Provide Guidance: Success stories often offer valuable insights and lessons learned. By learning from the experiences of others, we can avoid common pitfalls and make more informed decisions.

Foster a Sense of Community: Sharing success stories can create a sense of connection and belonging. It reminds us that we are not alone in our struggles and that there is support available to help us on our journey.

ᐳᐳᐳ

How to Share Success Stories Effectively

Find Authentic Stories: Look for genuine and inspiring stories that resonate with your audience.

Focus on the Journey: Highlight the challenges and obstacles that the individual overcame. This makes the story more relatable and inspiring.

Share Personal Connections: Whenever possible, connect the story to your own experiences or the experiences of your audience.

Keep it Concise and Engaging: Tell the story in a clear, concise, and engaging manner.

Use Visuals: Incorporate images or videos to make the story more impactful.

Create a Platform for Sharing: Encourage others to share their own success stories within your community.

ᐳᐳᐳ

The Benefits of Sharing Your Own Success

Sharing your own success stories can also be incredibly rewarding. It can:

Boost Your Own Confidence: Sharing your achievements can help you recognize and appreciate your own accomplishments.

Inspire Others: Your story may inspire others to pursue their own dreams and overcome their own challenges.

Build Your Reputation: Sharing your successes can help you build your credibility and establish yourself as a leader or expert in your field.

Sharing success stories is a powerful way to motivate and inspire others. By sharing our own triumphs and celebrating the achievements of others, we can create a more positive and supportive environment that encourages growth and personal development.

ᐳᐳᐳ

EIGHTY-TWO

ENCOURAGE COLLABORATION—IT FOSTERS COLLECTIVE ACHIEVEMENT

In today's complex world, achieving significant goals rarely happens in isolation. Collaboration, the act of working together towards a shared objective, is becoming increasingly crucial for individuals and organizations alike.

The Power of Collaboration

When we collaborate, we:

<u>Leverage Diverse Perspectives</u>: Bringing together people with different backgrounds, skills, and experiences leads to more creative and innovative solutions.

<u>Pool Resources and Expertise</u>: By combining our strengths, we can tackle challenges more effectively and efficiently.

<u>Increase Productivity</u>: Working together can often lead to increased productivity and faster results.

<u>Boost Motivation</u>: Collaboration can be highly motivating. Working with others can provide a sense of community, support, and shared purpose.

<u>Enhance Learning</u>: Collaborating with others provides opportunities to learn from each other, share knowledge, and develop new skills.

♭♭♭

How to Encourage Collaboration

<u>Foster Open Communication</u>: Create an environment where open and honest communication is valued and encouraged.

<u>Build Trust and Respect</u>: Cultivate a culture of trust and respect among team members.

<u>Encourage Shared Goals</u>: Clearly define shared goals and objectives that everyone understands and agrees upon.

<u>Provide Opportunities for Collaboration</u>: Create opportunities for team members to work together, such as group projects, brainstorming sessions, and cross-functional teams.

<u>Recognize and Reward Collaboration</u>: Acknowledge and reward collaborative efforts and achievements.

<u>Use Collaboration Tools</u>: Utilize technology to facilitate collaboration, such as project management software, online communication tools, and shared workspaces.

ppp

The Benefits of Collaborative Achievements

Collaborative achievements are often more meaningful and rewarding than individual accomplishments. They:

<u>Strengthen Relationships</u>: Collaboration builds stronger relationships among team members, fostering a sense of camaraderie and trust.

<u>Increase Job Satisfaction</u>: Working together on a successful project can be incredibly rewarding and satisfying.

<u>Boost Organizational Success</u>: Collaborative efforts can lead to significant improvements in organizational performance and competitiveness.

Collaboration is not just a nice-to-have; it's essential for success in today's interconnected world. By encouraging collaboration and creating an environment that supports teamwork, we can achieve greater things both individually and collectively.

ppp

EIGHTY-THREE
RECOGNIZE POTENTIAL IN PEOPLE BEFORE THEY SEE IT THEMSELVES

We all have hidden talents and untapped potential. But sometimes, we need a little nudge, a bit of encouragement, to realize our own capabilities. That's where the power of recognizing potential in others comes in.

The Importance of Seeing Potential

When you see potential in someone, you're essentially saying:

"I believe in you." This simple act of belief can be incredibly powerful. It can boost someone's self-confidence and motivate them to strive for greater things.

"You have more to offer." Recognizing potential helps individuals tap into their inner resources and discover abilities they may not have been aware of.

"I see your strengths." By highlighting their strengths and unique qualities, you help individuals understand their value and build on their existing skills.

How to Recognize Potential

Recognizing potential is about more than just gut feelings. Here are a few tips:

Pay Attention: Observe people's behavior, listen to their conversations, and notice their interests and passions.

<u>Look Beyond the Obvious</u>: Don't just focus on their current skills or accomplishments. Look for signs of curiosity, creativity, resilience, and a willingness to learn.

<u>Provide Challenging Opportunities</u>: Give people opportunities to step outside their comfort zones and try new things.

<u>Offer Constructive Feedback</u>: Provide honest and constructive feedback that focuses on their strengths and areas for growth.

<u>Encourage and Support</u>: Offer encouragement and support throughout their journey of self-discovery and growth.

ᐅᐅᐅ

The Impact of Recognizing Potential

When you recognize potential in others, you:

Empower individuals: You help them unlock their full potential and achieve their dreams. 1

<u>Empowering Potential</u>: The Power of Perception in Leadership | by Fayaz King | Medium

medium.com

<u>Foster growth</u>: You create an environment that encourages learning, innovation, and personal development.

<u>Build strong relationships</u>: Recognizing potential strengthens relationships and fosters a sense of trust and respect.

<u>Make a positive impact</u>: You contribute to the growth and development of individuals and the community as a whole.

Recognizing potential in others is a gift. It's about seeing the spark within someone and helping them ignite it. By believing in others and encouraging their growth, we can create a world where everyone has the opportunity to reach their full potential.

ᐅᐅᐅ

EIGHTY-FOUR

INSPIRE WITH QUESTIONS THAT SPARK CREATIVE THINKING

We all have the capacity for creative thinking, but sometimes it needs a little spark to ignite. One of the most powerful tools to unlock our creative potential is the right question.

The Power of Questioning

Questions have an incredible ability to:

Challenge Assumptions: They force us to step outside our comfort zones and question the status quo.

Stimulate Curiosity: They ignite our natural curiosity and encourage us to explore new ideas and possibilities.

Encourage Deeper Thinking: They push us to delve deeper into a topic and consider different perspectives.

Foster Collaboration: They create a space for open dialogue and encourage the sharing of ideas.

Asking the Right Questions

To spark creative thinking, focus on questions that are:

Open-ended: Avoid yes/no questions. Instead, ask questions that begin with "how," "why," "what if," and "imagine."

Provocative: Challenge existing beliefs and encourage unconventional thinking.

<u>Thought-provoking</u>: Encourage deep reflection and exploration of complex ideas.

<u>Action-oriented</u>: Inspire action and motivate individuals to pursue new ideas.

ᗐᗐᗐ

Examples of Creative Thinking Questions:

"What if we could...?" This classic question encourages out-of-the-box thinking and allows for limitless possibilities.

"How might we...?" This question focuses on finding solutions to a specific problem or challenge.

"What would happen if...?" This question encourages exploration of different scenarios and their potential outcomes.

"What are some unexpected uses for...?" This question encourages thinking outside the traditional boundaries of an object or concept.

Cultivating a Culture of Questioning

To foster a culture of creative thinking, it's important to:

<u>Encourage curiosity</u>: Create a safe and supportive environment where questions are valued and encouraged.

<u>Practice active listening</u>: Pay attention to the questions that others are asking and engage in meaningful dialogue.

Embrace "why" questions: Encourage individuals to question assumptions and seek deeper understanding.

<u>Celebrate creative thinking</u>: Recognize and reward individuals for their creative ideas and contributions.

Asking the right questions can unlock a world of creative possibilities. By cultivating a culture of questioning and embracing the power of inquiry.

We can inspire innovation, drive progress, and achieve our full potential.

ᗐᗐᗐ

EIGHTY-FIVE

SPEAK TO THE HEART BEFORE APPEALING TO THE MIND—IT CONNECTS DEEPLY

In our fast-paced world, we often prioritize logic and reason. We strive for data-driven decisions and rely heavily on facts and figures. However, true connection and lasting impact often come from a different place: the heart.

The Power of Emotion

Emotions are powerful drivers of human behavior. They influence our decisions, shape our relationships, and ultimately define our experiences. When we speak to the heart, we tap into these emotions, creating a deeper and more meaningful connection with our audience.

<u>Building Empathy</u>: By sharing stories and evoking emotions like joy, sadness, or anger, we can build empathy and understanding with our audience. We can help them see the world from a different perspective and connect with the human experience.

<u>Creating Meaning</u>: Appealing to the heart helps us connect with our audience on a deeper level. It allows us to create meaning and purpose, and to inspire action.

<u>Driving Action</u>: Emotions can be powerful motivators. When we tap into our audience's emotions, we can inspire them to take action, whether it's making a purchase, supporting a cause, or simply changing their perspective.

ᚦᚦᚦ

How to Speak to the Heart

<u>Tell Stories</u>: Stories are powerful tools for connecting with others on an emotional level. They allow us to share experiences, convey emotions, and create lasting memories.

<u>Use Emotional Language</u>: Use vivid language and imagery to evoke emotions in your audience.

<u>Be Authentic</u>: Authenticity is key. Be genuine and honest in your communication, and let your own emotions shine through.

<u>Focus on Values</u>: Connect with your audience's values and beliefs.

<u>Show Empathy</u>: Demonstrate that you understand and care about your audience's feelings and experiences.

ᚦᚦᚦ

Finding the Balance

While appealing to the heart is crucial, it's important to find the right balance. While emotions are powerful, logic and reason also play a vital role in decision-making.

By combining emotional appeals with sound logic and data, you can create a compelling and persuasive message.

Speaking to the heart is not about manipulating emotions or being disingenuous. It's about connecting with others on a deeper level, building empathy, and creating meaningful experiences.

By understanding the power of emotion and learning to communicate with the heart, we can build stronger relationships, inspire action, and make a lasting impact on the world.

ᚦᚦᚦ

EIGHTY-SIX

USE STORYTELLING TO CONVEY LESSONS AND INSPIRE CHANGE

Stories have been a part of the human experience for millennia. From ancient cave paintings to modern-day movies, we have always used stories to entertain, to inform, and to connect with each other. But stories have a power that goes beyond mere entertainment: they can convey powerful lessons and inspire profound change.

The Power of Storytelling

Making Complex Ideas Understandable: Stories can make complex ideas and abstract concepts more accessible and engaging. By weaving information into a narrative, we can make it more relatable and memorable.

Inspiring Empathy and Understanding: Stories can help us understand the perspectives and experiences of others. By stepping into the shoes of a fictional character or learning about the struggles and triumphs of real people, we can develop empathy and compassion.

Driving Action and Change: Stories can inspire us to take action. Whether it's fighting for social justice, protecting the environment, or simply making a positive impact on our own lives, stories can motivate us to make a difference.

Transmitting Cultural Values: Stories are powerful vehicles for transmitting cultural values and traditions from one generation to the next. They help us understand our history, our identity, and our place in the world.

ᗦᗦᗦ

Using Storytelling to Inspire Change

<u>Share Personal Stories</u>: Sharing your own personal stories can be incredibly powerful. It can help others understand your experiences, connect with you on a deeper level, and inspire them to take action.

<u>Tell Stories of Hope and Resilience</u>: Stories of overcoming adversity, achieving great things, and making a positive impact on the world can be incredibly inspiring.

<u>Use Storytelling to Raise Awareness</u>: Stories can help raise awareness about important social and environmental issues. By sharing the stories of those affected by these issues, we can inspire action and create positive change.

<u>Incorporate Storytelling into Education</u>: Storytelling can be a powerful tool for teaching and learning. By incorporating stories into the classroom, we can make learning more engaging and memorable.

Stories have the power to change the world. They can inspire us, educate us, and connect us with each other on a deeper level.

By embracing the power of storytelling, we can create a more compassionate, just, and equitable world for all.

ᗦᗦᗦ

EIGHTY-SEVEN

REMIND OTHERS OF THEIR PROGRESS—IT FUELS PERSEVERANCE

We all face challenges on our journeys towards our goals. Whether it's learning a new skill, starting a business, or simply improving our health, setbacks and moments of doubt are inevitable. During these times, it's easy to lose sight of how far we've come and focus solely on what's left to achieve. This is where the power of acknowledging progress comes in.

The Importance of Acknowledging Progress

When we remind others (and ourselves) of the progress they've made, we:

Boost Motivation: Acknowledging achievements, no matter how small, reinforces the belief that progress is possible and motivates individuals to keep going.

Increase Confidence: Recognizing accomplishments builds confidence and self-esteem. It helps individuals believe in their abilities and overcome self-doubt.

Foster Perseverance: When individuals see tangible evidence of their progress, they are more likely to persevere through challenges and setbacks.

Strengthen Relationships: Acknowledging the progress of others strengthens relationships by showing support, appreciation, and genuine care.

❦❦❦

How to Acknowledge Progress Effectively

Be Specific: Instead of generic praise, be specific about the progress made. For example, instead of saying "You're doing great," say "I'm impressed with how consistently you've been practicing the piano lately."

Focus on Effort and Growth: Acknowledge the effort and dedication that has led to the progress, not just the outcome.

Celebrate Milestones: Celebrate both big and small milestones along the way. These celebrations provide a sense of accomplishment and keep motivation high.

Offer Encouragement: Offer words of encouragement and support, reminding individuals of their strengths and resilience.

ᐅᐅᐅ

The Benefits of Acknowledging Your Own Progress

Acknowledging your own progress is equally important. By reflecting on your achievements, you:

Maintain Motivation: Regularly acknowledging your progress helps you stay motivated and focused on your goals.

Build Self-Confidence: Recognizing your accomplishments boosts your self-confidence and reinforces your belief in your abilities.

Learn and Grow: Reflecting on your progress allows you to identify areas of improvement and learn from your successes and failures.

Acknowledging progress, both in ourselves and in others, is a powerful tool for fostering motivation, building confidence, and cultivating a growth mindset.

By celebrating achievements and reminding individuals of how far they've come, we can empower them to persevere through challenges and achieve their full potential.

ᐅᐅᐅ

EIGHTY-EIGHT

EMPOWER OTHERS TO TAKE OWNERSHIP—IT BUILDS CONFIDENCE

Imagine a world where everyone feels confident in their abilities and takes pride in their work. This isn't a fantasy; it's a reality we can create by empowering others to take ownership.

The Power of Ownership

When we empower others to take ownership, we:

Boost Confidence: Taking ownership of tasks, projects, and decisions fosters a sense of responsibility and accomplishment. This, in turn, boosts self-confidence and encourages individuals to step outside their comfort zones.

Increase Motivation: When people feel invested in something, they are more motivated to put in the effort and see it through to completion. Ownership breeds a sense of purpose and drives individuals to strive for excellence.

Foster Independence: Empowering others to take ownership encourages independence and self-reliance. It helps individuals develop the skills and confidence to navigate challenges and make their own decisions.

Promote Innovation: When people feel empowered to take ownership, they are more likely to think creatively and come up with innovative solutions.

ppp

How to Empower Others to Take Ownership

<u>Delegate Effectively</u>: Delegate tasks and responsibilities thoughtfully, considering individual strengths and interests.

<u>Provide Clear Expectations</u>: Clearly communicate goals, deadlines, and expectations.

<u>Offer Support and Guidance</u>: Provide the necessary support and guidance while allowing individuals the freedom to explore and experiment.

<u>Encourage Decision-Making</u>: Encourage individuals to make their own decisions and take responsibility for the outcomes.

<u>Provide Constructive Feedback</u>: Offer regular and constructive feedback that focuses on both strengths and areas for improvement.

<u>Celebrate Successes</u>: Acknowledge and celebrate individual and team successes.

ᗡᗡᗡ

The Benefits of Empowering Others

Empowering others to take ownership brings numerous benefits:

<u>Increased Productivity</u>: Empowered individuals are more productive and efficient in their work.

<u>Improved Teamwork</u>: A culture of ownership fosters stronger teamwork and collaboration.

<u>Enhanced Innovation</u>: Empowered individuals are more likely to come up with creative solutions and drive innovation.

<u>Stronger Leadership</u>: Empowering others to take ownership develops strong leaders within the organization.

Empowering others to take ownership is not just about delegating tasks; it's about fostering a culture of trust, respect, and shared responsibility.

By empowering others to take ownership of their work and their own development, we can create a more confident, motivated, and successful workforce.

ᗡᗡᗡ

EIGHTY-NINE

ADDRESS FEARS AND OFFER REASSURANCE—IT STRENGTHENS RESOLVE

Fear is a natural human emotion. It's a primal instinct designed to protect us from danger. However, when unchecked, fear can paralyze us, preventing us from pursuing our goals and living our lives to the fullest. That's why it's crucial to address fears and offer reassurance – it strengthens our resolve and empowers us to overcome obstacles.

The Impact of Unaddressed Fears

When we allow fear to dominate our thoughts and actions, it can:

Hinder Progress: Fear can lead to procrastination, avoidance, and ultimately, the failure to achieve our goals.

Damage Self-Confidence: Constant worry and anxiety can erode our self-confidence and make us doubt our abilities.

Strain Relationships: Fear can create tension and distance in our relationships, both personal and professional.

Impede Growth: Fear can prevent us from taking risks, trying new things, and stepping outside of our comfort zones, thus hindering our personal and professional growth.

ᐅᐅᐅ

Addressing Fears and Offering Reassurance

To overcome fear and strengthen our resolve, we can:

Acknowledge and Validate Fears: Instead of ignoring or suppressing our fears, we should acknowledge and validate them. Recognizing our fears is the first step towards overcoming them.

Challenge Negative Thoughts: Often, our fears are based on negative and unrealistic thoughts. By challenging these thoughts and replacing them with more positive and realistic ones, we can reframe our perspective.

Break Down Challenges: Large goals can seem daunting and overwhelming. Breaking them down into smaller, more manageable steps can make them feel less intimidating and more achievable.

Focus on Strengths and Past Successes: Remembering our past successes and focusing on our strengths can boost our confidence and remind us of our resilience.

Seek Support: Talking to trusted friends, family members, or mentors can provide valuable support and encouragement.

ᐅᐅᐅ

The Power of Reassurance

Offering reassurance to others can have a profound impact. When we believe in someone's abilities and encourage them to overcome their fears, we empower them to achieve great things. Reassurance can:

Boost Confidence: Knowing that someone believes in you can significantly boost your self-confidence and motivation.

Reduce Anxiety: Reassurance can help alleviate anxiety and reduce the impact of fear.

Encourage Risk-Taking: With the support of others, individuals are more likely to take risks and step outside of their comfort zones.

Addressing fears and offering reassurance are essential for personal and professional growth. By acknowledging our fears, challenging negative thoughts, and seeking support, we can overcome obstacles and achieve our goals. Moreover, by offering reassurance to others, we can empower them to reach their full potential.

ᐅᐅᐅ

NINETY

SET HIGH EXPECTATIONS—IT CHALLENGES PEOPLE TO RISE ABOVE

We all need a little push sometimes. Whether it's at work, school, or even in our personal lives, having high expectations for ourselves and others can be incredibly motivating.

The Power of High Expectations

When we set high expectations:

We unlock potential: High expectations push people to strive for more than they thought possible. They challenge individuals to reach beyond their comfort zones and discover hidden talents and abilities.

We foster growth: Setting high expectations encourages continuous learning and improvement. It motivates individuals to develop new skills, overcome challenges, and achieve greater things.

We build confidence: As individuals meet and exceed high expectations, their self-confidence soars. They realize their own potential and develop a strong belief in their abilities.

We create a culture of excellence: High expectations create a culture of excellence where everyone strives for their best. This leads to improved performance, increased productivity, and greater overall success.

ϧϧϧ

Setting High Expectations Effectively

<u>Be Clear and Specific</u>: Clearly communicate expectations and ensure everyone understands what is expected of them.

<u>Provide Support and Guidance</u>: Offer the necessary support and guidance to help individuals achieve their goals.

<u>Focus on Growth, Not Just Results</u>: Emphasize the importance of learning and growth, not just the final outcome.

<u>Celebrate Successes</u>: Acknowledge and celebrate achievements, no matter how small. This reinforces the positive impact of high expectations and motivates individuals to continue striving for excellence.

<u>Be Patient and Understanding</u>: Understand that it takes time and effort to meet high expectations. Be patient and understanding, and offer encouragement along the way.

ppp

The Importance of Self-Expectations

Setting high expectations for ourselves is equally important. When we believe in our own abilities and strive for excellence, we are more likely to achieve our goals and live a fulfilling life.

Setting high expectations is not about being unrealistic or overly demanding. It's about believing in the potential of others and ourselves, and creating an environment that encourages growth, innovation, and excellence.

By setting high expectations and providing the necessary support, we can empower individuals to achieve their full potential and reach new heights.

ppp

NINETY-ONE

ACKNOWLEDGE EFFORT, NOT JUST RESULTS—IT ENCOURAGES PERSISTENCE

We often focus on the outcome, on achieving the goal. While success is important, it's crucial to remember that the journey itself is equally valuable. Acknowledging and appreciating the effort put in, regardless of the final result, is key to fostering perseverance and a growth mindset.

The Power of Acknowledging Effort

When we acknowledge effort:

<u>We Build Resilience</u>: Recognizing the dedication and hard work that goes into any endeavor helps individuals develop resilience. They learn that setbacks are temporary and that persistent effort will eventually lead to progress.

<u>We Foster a Growth Mindset</u>: Focusing on effort shifts the emphasis from outcomes to the learning process. Individuals understand that mistakes are opportunities for growth and that continuous improvement is more important than perfection.

<u>We Increase Motivation</u>: Knowing that their efforts are valued and appreciated motivates individuals to keep striving, even when faced with

challenges.

<u>We Strengthen Relationships</u>: Acknowledging the effort of others strengthens relationships by demonstrating respect, appreciation, and genuine care.

ᗧᗧᗧ

How to Acknowledge Effort Effectively

<u>Be Specific</u>: Instead of generic praise, be specific about the effort made. For example, instead of saying "You did a good job," say "I really appreciate the time and effort you put into researching this topic."

<u>Focus on the Process</u>: Highlight the dedication, perseverance, and problem-solving skills demonstrated throughout the process.

<u>Offer Constructive Feedback</u>: Provide constructive feedback that focuses on both strengths and areas for improvement.

<u>Celebrate Learning</u>: Acknowledge the lessons learned, even from setbacks.

ᗧᗧᗧ

The Benefits of Acknowledging Your Own Effort

Acknowledging your own effort is equally important. By recognizing and appreciating the hard work you put in, you:

<u>Boost Self-Esteem</u>: Acknowledging your own efforts reinforces your self-worth and builds self-confidence.

<u>Maintain Motivation</u>: Recognizing your dedication keeps you motivated and inspired to continue striving towards your goals.

<u>Develop a Growth Mindset</u>: Acknowledging your effort helps you focus on the learning process and embrace challenges as opportunities for growth.

Acknowledging effort, not just results, is crucial for fostering a culture of growth and perseverance. By recognizing and appreciating the dedication and hard work of others (and ourselves), we create an environment where individuals feel valued, motivated, and empowered to reach their full potential.

ᗧᗧᗧ

NINETY-TWO

SHOW VULNERABILITY—IT MAKES YOU RELATABLE AND AUTHENTIC

In our hyper-connected world, we often present a curated version of ourselves online and in person. We strive for perfection, fearing judgment and rejection. But this pursuit of an "immaculate" image can leave us feeling isolated, disconnected, and ultimately, inauthentic. This is where the courage of vulnerability comes in.

Vulnerability, often perceived as a weakness, is actually a powerful tool for building deeper connections, fostering empathy, and ultimately, living a more authentic and fulfilling life.

The Myths of Vulnerability

Myth 1: Vulnerability is weakness: This is a common misconception. True vulnerability requires strength and courage. It takes courage to acknowledge our fears, insecurities, and imperfections.

Myth 2: Vulnerability makes you weak: On the contrary, vulnerability can actually make us stronger. By acknowledging our limitations, we can identify areas for growth and develop resilience.

Myth 3: Vulnerability will be exploited: While there is always a risk of vulnerability being misused, building trust and choosing who we share our vulnerabilities with is crucial.

♭♭♭

The Benefits of Embracing Vulnerability

<u>Deeper Connections</u>: When we share our fears, insecurities, and imperfections, we open ourselves up to deeper levels of connection with others. It allows others to see us as human, with all our flaws and imperfections. This fosters genuine intimacy and strengthens relationships.

<u>Increased Empathy</u>: By sharing our vulnerabilities, we encourage others to share theirs. This creates a sense of empathy and understanding, allowing us to connect with others on a deeper, more human level.

<u>Enhanced Authenticity</u>: Embracing vulnerability allows us to live more authentically. We no longer have to pretend to be someone we are not, freeing us from the burden of maintaining a perfect facade.

<u>Increased Trust</u>: When we are willing to be vulnerable, we demonstrate that we are authentic and trustworthy. This builds trust with others and fosters stronger, more meaningful relationships.

<u>Personal Growth</u>: Vulnerability encourages personal growth. By acknowledging our weaknesses and seeking support, we can identify areas for improvement, overcome challenges, and develop resilience.

ppp

How to Cultivate Vulnerability

<u>Start Small</u>: Begin by sharing small, manageable vulnerabilities with trusted friends or family members.

<u>Choose the Right Setting</u>: Share your vulnerabilities in a safe and supportive environment.

<u>Be Intentional</u>: Share your vulnerabilities with the intention of building deeper connections, not seeking pity or attention.

<u>Practice Self-Compassion</u>: Be kind and compassionate to yourself as you navigate the process of vulnerability.

<u>Focus on Your Values</u>: Align your vulnerabilities with your values. Share what matters most to you, even if it makes you feel exposed.

Embracing vulnerability is a journey, not a destination. It requires courage, self-awareness, and a willingness to be authentic. But the rewards are immense. By embracing vulnerability, we can build deeper connections, live more authentically, and experience a greater sense of freedom and fulfillment.

ppp

NINETY-THREE

USE METAPHORS TO SIMPLIFY COMPLEX IDEAS—IT CREATES CLARITY

Imagine trying to explain the intricate workings of a clock to a child. You could delve into the mechanics of gears, springs, and pendulums, but chances are, they'd glaze over. Instead, you might say, "It's like a tiny orchestra, with each part playing its own tune to make the music of time."

This simple metaphor, comparing a clock to an orchestra, suddenly makes the complex seem familiar. This is the power of metaphors – to bridge the gap between the abstract and the concrete, making complex ideas easier to grasp.

The Magic of Metaphors

Metaphors are figures of speech that compare two seemingly unrelated things, highlighting a shared characteristic. They work by:

<u>Creating Vivid Imagery</u>: Metaphors paint pictures in our minds, making abstract concepts more tangible and memorable. "Life is a journey," for example, evokes images of travel, with its twists and turns, unexpected detours, and eventual destination.

<u>Simplifying Complexity</u>: By comparing a complex idea to something familiar, metaphors break down barriers to understanding. They allow us to grasp intricate concepts by relating them to everyday experiences.

Engaging Emotion: Metaphors can evoke emotions and create a deeper connection with the audience. "Love is a battlefield," for instance, conveys the intensity and challenges of romantic relationships.

Making Information Memorable: Metaphors are highly memorable. They create a lasting impression by associating abstract concepts with vivid imagery and relatable experiences.

ᗡᗡᗡ

Using Metaphors Effectively

Choose the Right Metaphor: Select metaphors that are relevant to your audience and the context of your message.

Keep it Simple: Avoid overly complex or obscure metaphors that might confuse your audience.

Use Metaphors Sparingly: Overuse of metaphors can dilute their impact. Use them strategically to emphasize key points.

Consider Your Audience: Tailor your metaphors to your audience's background and knowledge.

ᗡᗡᗡ

The Benefits of Metaphorical Thinking

Beyond communication, metaphors can enhance our own thinking and problem-solving abilities. By viewing problems from different perspectives and making unexpected connections, we can unlock new insights and generate creative solutions.

Metaphors are a powerful tool for simplifying complex ideas, enhancing understanding, and fostering creativity. By harnessing the power of metaphors.

We can communicate more effectively, deepen our understanding of the world around us, and unlock new avenues of thought and imagination.

ᗡᗡᗡ

NINETY-FOUR

ENCOURAGE PEOPLE TO DREAM BIG—IT EXPANDS POSSIBILITIES

In a world that often emphasizes practicality and playing it safe, dreaming big can seem like a frivolous pursuit. Yet, the power of big dreams cannot be underestimated. They ignite our imaginations, fuel our passions, and ultimately expand the realm of what we believe is possible.

The Magic of Big Dreams

Big dreams are more than just fantasies; they are seeds of possibility. They:

<u>Ignite Passion and Purpose</u>: When we dream big, we tap into our deepest desires and passions. These dreams give our lives direction and purpose, providing a sense of meaning and motivation.

<u>Expand Our Horizons</u>: Big dreams push us beyond our comfort zones, encouraging us to explore new ideas, embrace challenges, and discover hidden talents and abilities. They broaden our perspectives and open us up to new possibilities.

<u>Foster Creativity and Innovation</u>: Dreaming big allows us to think outside the box, challenge conventional wisdom, and come up with innovative solutions to problems.

<u>Build Resilience</u>: The pursuit of big dreams inevitably involves setbacks and obstacles. Overcoming these challenges builds resilience, perseverance, and a strong sense of self-belief.

<u>Inspire Others</u>: When we share our big dreams with others, we inspire them to dream big too. We create a ripple effect of hope, possibility, and collective action.

ԲԲԲ

How to Encourage Big Dreams

<u>Foster Curiosity</u>: Encourage a sense of wonder and curiosity in yourself and others. Ask "what if?" questions and explore the unknown.

<u>Embrace Imagination</u>: Create a safe space for imagination and creativity to flourish. Encourage children to play, daydream, and explore their inner worlds.

<u>Celebrate Ambitions</u>: Acknowledge and celebrate ambitious goals, no matter how seemingly unattainable.

<u>Provide Support and Guidance</u>: Offer support and guidance to those pursuing their big dreams. Help them break down their goals into smaller, more manageable steps.

<u>Share Your Own Dreams</u>: Share your own big dreams with others. Your own example can inspire and motivate others to pursue their aspirations.

Dreaming big is not about escaping reality; it's about creating a vision for a better future. It's about believing in the power of human potential and striving for something extraordinary. By encouraging ourselves and others to dream big, we unlock a world of possibilities and pave the way for a brighter future.

ԲԲԲ

NINETY-FIVE

SHARE YOUR "WHY"—IT ADDS MEANING TO THE JOURNEY

We all have goals, ambitions, and dreams. But what truly drives us? What gives us the strength to persevere through challenges and setbacks? Often, it's our "why"—the underlying reason, the deeper purpose, that fuels our journey.

The Power of "Why"

Our "why" is the core motivation behind our actions. It's the answer to the question, "Why am I doing this?" When we understand our "why," we:

<u>Find Deeper Meaning</u>: Connecting our actions to a deeper purpose adds meaning and significance to our journey. It transforms mundane tasks into meaningful pursuits.

<u>Increase Motivation</u>: Knowing our "why" provides a powerful source of intrinsic motivation. It fuels our perseverance, even when faced with obstacles.

<u>Enhance Resilience</u>: When we understand the deeper meaning behind our efforts, we are more likely to bounce back from setbacks. Our "why" provides the strength to keep going, even when things get tough.

<u>Improve Decision-Making</u>: Our "why" acts as a guiding compass, helping us make decisions that align with our values and purpose.

<u>Connect with Others</u>: Sharing our "why" with others can build deeper connections. It allows us to share our passions and inspire others to pursue their own dreams.

ᕯᕯᕯ

Discovering Your "Why"

Discovering your "why" is a deeply personal journey. Here are a few questions to help you uncover your deeper purpose:

What are my values? What is truly important to me? What principles guide my decisions?

What makes me feel fulfilled? What activities bring me joy and a sense of purpose?

What impact do I want to make on the world? How can I use my talents and skills to make a difference?

What legacy do I want to leave behind? What do I want to be remembered for?

Sharing Your "Why"

Sharing your "why" with others can be incredibly powerful. It:

<u>Inspires Others</u>: Sharing your passion and purpose can inspire others to pursue their own dreams.

<u>Builds Community</u>: Connecting with others who share similar values and passions can create a strong sense of community and support.

Strengthens Your Resolve: Articulating your "why" can help you stay focused and committed to your goals.

Discovering and sharing your "why" is a crucial step in living a meaningful and fulfilling life. It provides a sense of purpose, fuels our motivation, and empowers us to overcome challenges. By understanding what truly drives us, we can align our actions with our values and make a lasting impact on the world.

ᕯᕯᕯ

NINETY-SIX

HIGHLIGHT THE IMPACT OF THEIR WORK—IT BOOSTS MORALE

In any workplace, it's easy to get caught up in the daily grind. The constant stream of tasks, deadlines, and meetings can sometimes make it feel like our efforts are going unnoticed. However, recognizing and highlighting the impact of each individual's work is crucial for boosting morale, fostering a positive work environment, and motivating employees to excel.

The Power of Recognition

When we acknowledge and appreciate the impact of someone's work, we:

<u>Boost Morale</u>: Recognizing the value of individual contributions boosts employee morale and creates a sense of purpose and accomplishment.

<u>Increase Motivation</u>: Knowing that their work is valued and appreciated motivates employees to work harder and strive for excellence.

<u>Foster a Positive Work Environment</u>: A culture of recognition fosters a positive and supportive work environment where employees feel valued and appreciated.

<u>Improve Employee Engagement</u>: When employees feel valued and appreciated, they are more engaged in their work and more likely to go the extra mile.

<u>Enhance Performance</u>: Recognizing and celebrating accomplishments encourages employees to continue improving their skills and exceeding

expectations.

ᗊᗊᗊ

How to Highlight the Impact of Work

<u>Be Specific</u>: Instead of generic praise, be specific about the impact of their work. For example, instead of saying "You did a great job," say "Your presentation was incredibly insightful and helped the team secure the deal."

<u>Connect Work to the Bigger Picture</u>: Explain how an individual's contribution contributes to the overall success of the team and the organization.

<u>Publicly Acknowledge Achievements</u>: Publicly acknowledge and celebrate employee achievements through company newsletters, team meetings, or social media.

<u>Offer Rewards and Recognition</u>: Consider offering rewards and recognition programs to acknowledge outstanding contributions.

<u>Provide Feedback Regularly</u>: Regularly provide constructive feedback that highlights both strengths and areas for improvement.

ᗊᗊᗊ

The Benefits of Acknowledging Your Own Impact

It's equally important to acknowledge the impact of your own work. By reflecting on your accomplishments and recognizing the value you bring, you:

<u>Boost Self-Confidence</u>: Acknowledging your own impact boosts your self-esteem and reinforces your belief in your abilities.

<u>Increase Motivation</u>: Recognizing your own contributions keeps you motivated and inspired to continue striving for excellence.

<u>Identify Areas for Growth</u>: Reflecting on your impact allows you to identify areas for improvement and develop new skills.

Highlighting the impact of work is not just about saying "thank you." It's about recognizing the value of each individual contribution, fostering a culture of appreciation, and creating a workplace where employees feel valued, motivated, and empowered to excel.

By acknowledging the impact of their work, we can create a more positive and productive work environment for everyone.

ᗊᗊᗊ

NINETY-SEVEN

BE GENUINE AND SINCERE—IT BUILDS TRUST AND LOYALTY

In a world that often prioritizes appearances and superficiality, genuine sincerity stands out. It's the bedrock of strong relationships, whether personal or professional. When we are genuine and sincere, we communicate honestly, act with integrity, and build trust that lasts.

The Power of Authenticity

Being genuine is about being true to yourself. It's about expressing your authentic self, with your thoughts, feelings, and beliefs. When we are genuine:

We Build Trust: Authenticity fosters trust. When people see that we are being honest and transparent, they are more likely to trust us and our intentions.

We Strengthen Relationships: Genuine connections are built on honesty and authenticity. When we are sincere with others, we deepen our relationships and build stronger bonds.

We Increase Our Credibility: Being genuine enhances our credibility. When people see that we are authentic and trustworthy, they are more likely to believe in us and our words.

We Reduce Stress: Trying to maintain a facade can be exhausting. Being genuine allows us to be ourselves, reducing stress and increasing overall well-being.

<u>We Inspire Others</u>: When we are genuine, we inspire others to be authentic as well. We create a ripple effect of authenticity, encouraging others to be true to themselves.

ᕬᕬᕬ

Cultivating Genuine Sincerity

<u>Practice Self-Awareness</u>: Increase your self-awareness by reflecting on your thoughts, feelings, and values.

<u>Be Honest with Yourself</u>: Acknowledge your strengths and weaknesses. Be honest with yourself about your motivations and intentions.

<u>Communicate Openly and Honestly</u>: Express your thoughts and feelings openly and honestly, while being mindful of the feelings of others.

<u>Listen Actively</u>: Truly listen to others and try to understand their perspectives.

<u>Be Consistent</u>: Your words and actions should align. Be consistent in your behavior and demonstrate integrity in all your interactions.

In a world that often values appearances over authenticity, genuine sincerity is a rare and valuable trait. By cultivating authenticity and embracing our true selves, we can build stronger relationships, increase our credibility, and live a more fulfilling and meaningful life.

ᕬᕬᕬ

NINETY-EIGHT

CREATE A SAFE SPACE FOR SHARING IDEAS—IT FOSTERS INNOVATION

Innovation thrives in environments where individuals feel comfortable expressing their unique perspectives and ideas without fear of judgment or criticism. Creating a safe space for idea sharing is crucial for unlocking creativity, fostering collaboration, and driving meaningful progress.

The Importance of Psychological Safety

A safe space, in this context, refers to an environment where individuals feel psychologically safe to:

<u>Express their opinions freely</u>: Share their thoughts and ideas openly, even if they are unconventional or unconventional.

<u>Take risks</u>: Experiment with new ideas and approaches without fear of failure.

<u>Ask questions</u>: Inquire about anything without feeling intimidated or judged.

<u>Challenge the status quo</u>: Question existing assumptions and propose alternative solutions.

<u>Learn from mistakes</u>: Acknowledge and learn from failures without fear of negative consequences.

ᖚᖚᖚ

Building a Safe Space for Idea Sharing

<u>Lead by Example</u>: Leaders must model the behavior they expect from others. Be open to new ideas, actively listen to others, and acknowledge and appreciate diverse perspectives.

<u>Encourage Open Communication</u>: Foster a culture of open and honest communication where all voices are heard and valued.

<u>Promote Psychological Safety</u>: Explicitly communicate the importance of psychological safety and actively work to create an environment where individuals feel comfortable taking risks.

<u>Minimize Fear of Failure</u>: Encourage experimentation and learning from mistakes. View failures as opportunities for growth and improvement.

<u>Celebrate Diversity of Thought</u>: Value and appreciate diverse perspectives and encourage individuals to challenge the status quo.

<u>Provide Constructive Feedback</u>: Provide constructive feedback that focuses on ideas and their potential, rather than personal criticism.

ppp

The Benefits of a Safe Space for Idea Sharing

When individuals feel safe to share their ideas, they are more likely to:

<u>Be more creative and innovative</u>: Feel empowered to think outside the box and come up with novel solutions.

<u>Take more risks</u>: Be willing to experiment with new ideas and approaches.

<u>Collaborate more effectively</u>: Work together more effectively to achieve common goals.

<u>Be more engaged and motivated</u>: Feel more invested in their work and more motivated to contribute.

<u>Grow and develop</u>: Learn and grow from feedback and challenges.

Creating a safe space for idea sharing is not just about avoiding criticism; it's about fostering an environment where individuals feel valued, respected, and empowered to contribute their unique perspectives. By cultivating a culture of psychological safety, we can unlock the full potential of our teams and drive innovation across all levels of our organizations.

ppp

NINETY-NINE

INSPIRE THROUGH ACTION—DEMONSTRATE THE BEHAVIORS YOU WANT TO SEE

Words often fall short when it comes to inspiring change. People are more likely to be influenced by what they see than what they hear. This is where the power of leading by example comes in. By demonstrating the behaviors you want to see in others, you can inspire positive change and create a lasting impact.

The Power of Action

Actions speak louder than words. When we consistently demonstrate the behaviors we wish to encourage, we:

<u>Build Trust and Credibility</u>: Our actions speak volumes about our values and beliefs. Consistent behavior builds trust and credibility, making others more likely to follow our lead.

<u>Inspire Motivation</u>: Seeing someone else embody the desired behaviors can be incredibly motivating. It shows others that the desired behaviors are achievable and attainable.

<u>Foster a Positive Environment</u>: When leaders and role models consistently demonstrate positive behaviors, they create a positive and supportive environment that encourages others to do the same.

<u>Promote a Culture of Change</u>: By consistently demonstrating the desired behaviors, we can help to create a culture of change within our

organizations, communities, and even within ourselves.

ᐅᐅᐅ

Leading by Example in Action

<u>Demonstrate Work Ethic</u>: Consistently arrive on time, meet deadlines, and put in the effort required to achieve goals.

<u>Prioritize Communication</u>: Practice clear and effective communication, both verbal and written. Actively listen to others and value their perspectives.

<u>Embrace Teamwork</u>: Collaborate effectively with others, support your colleagues, and celebrate team successes.

<u>Show Respect and Compassion</u>: Treat everyone with respect and compassion, regardless of their position or background.

<u>Embrace Continuous Learning</u>: Continuously seek opportunities to learn and grow, both personally and professionally.

ᐅᐅᐅ

The Impact of Leading by Example

Leading by example has a profound impact on those around us. It inspires others to strive for excellence, fosters a positive and supportive environment, and creates a lasting legacy of positive change.

Words can inspire, but actions speak volumes. By consistently demonstrating the behaviors we wish to see in others, we can inspire positive change, cultivate a culture of excellence, and create a lasting impact on the world around us.

ᐅᐅᐅ

ONE HUNDRED

OFFER HOPE DURING TOUGH TIMES—IT INSTILLS RESILIENCE

Life throws curveballs. Unexpected challenges, disappointments, and setbacks are inevitable. During these tough times, it's easy to feel lost, discouraged, and even hopeless. That's why offering hope is so crucial. A flicker of hope, a belief in a brighter future, can be a lifeline, providing the strength to persevere and emerge stronger from adversity.

The Power of Hope

Hope is not merely wishful thinking; it's a powerful force that:

Fosters Resilience: Hope acts as a buffer against despair. It gives us the strength to endure hardship, overcome obstacles, and bounce back from setbacks.

Motivates Action: Hope fuels our motivation. It encourages us to take action, to seek solutions, and to strive towards a better future.

Improves Well-being: Hope has a profound impact on our mental and emotional well-being. It reduces stress, anxiety, and depression, and promotes overall happiness.

Strengthens Relationships: Sharing hope with others builds stronger connections. It fosters a sense of community and support, reminding us that we are not alone in our struggles.

Inspires Change: Hope inspires us to strive for a better future, to work towards positive change, and to make a difference in the world.

ᛒᛒᛒ

Offering Hope to Others

<u>Listen with Empathy</u>: Actively listen to others' concerns and challenges without judgment.

<u>Offer Words of Encouragement</u>: Offer words of encouragement, support, and belief in their ability to overcome challenges.

<u>Share Stories of Hope</u>: Share stories of resilience, perseverance, and overcoming adversity.

<u>Focus on Solutions</u>: Help others identify potential solutions and develop a plan for moving forward.

<u>Be a Source of Support</u>: Be a source of support and encouragement, offering a helping hand and a listening ear.

ϸϸϸ

Cultivating Hope Within Yourself

It's equally important to cultivate hope within ourselves.

<u>Focus on Gratitude</u>: Practice gratitude by appreciating the good things in your life, no matter how small.

<u>Set Realistic Goals</u>: Set achievable goals and celebrate small victories along the way.

<u>Engage in Activities You Enjoy</u>: Spend time on activities that bring you joy and fulfillment.

<u>Connect with Nature</u>: Spend time in nature, which has been shown to have a positive impact on mental well-being.

<u>Practice Self-Compassion</u>: Be kind and compassionate to yourself, especially during challenging times.

Offering hope is an act of kindness and compassion. It's about believing in the potential of others, supporting them through difficult times, and inspiring them to keep moving forward. By offering hope to others and cultivating hope within ourselves, we can create a brighter future for ourselves and for those around us.

ϸϸϸ

ONE HUNDRED AND ONE

REMIND OTHERS OF THEIR UNIQUE STRENGTHS—IT INSPIRES SELF-BELIEF

We all possess a unique set of talents, skills, and qualities that make us who we are. However, in the hustle and bustle of daily life, it's easy to lose sight of these strengths. That's why it's crucial to remind others of their unique abilities – it's a powerful way to inspire self-belief and empower them to reach their full potential.

The Power of Recognition

When we acknowledge and celebrate the unique strengths of others:

<u>We Boost Self-Confidence</u>: Recognizing someone's talents and abilities validates their worth and boosts their self-esteem. It helps them believe in themselves and their capabilities.

<u>We Foster a Growth Mindset</u>: By highlighting their strengths, we encourage individuals to focus on their areas of excellence and embrace their unique gifts. This fosters a growth mindset, where individuals view challenges as opportunities for learning and improvement.

<u>We Encourage Self-Discovery</u>: Reminding others of their strengths encourages them to explore their talents further and discover new passions

and interests.

<u>We Strengthen Relationships</u>: Recognizing and appreciating the unique qualities of others strengthens relationships. It builds trust, fosters connection, and creates a more positive and supportive environment.

<u>We Inspire Action</u>: When individuals are aware of their strengths, they are more likely to use them to their advantage, pursue their passions, and achieve their goals.

ᐅᐅᐅ

How to Acknowledge Others' Strengths Effectively

<u>Be Specific</u>: Instead of generic praise, be specific about their strengths. For example, instead of saying "You're good at this," say "You have a remarkable ability to connect with people and build rapport."

Provide Concrete Examples: Provide specific examples of how they have demonstrated their strengths.

<u>Offer Encouragement</u>: Encourage individuals to utilize their strengths and explore their potential.

<u>Create a Supportive Environment</u>: Foster an environment where individuals feel safe and comfortable expressing themselves and showcasing their talents.

ᐅᐅᐅ

The Importance of Self-Reflection

It's equally important to remind ourselves of our own unique strengths.

<u>Practice Self-Reflection</u>: Regularly reflect on your accomplishments and identify your strengths.

<u>Celebrate Your Achievements</u>: Acknowledge and celebrate your successes, no matter how small.

<u>Focus on Your Unique Value</u>: Recognize what makes you unique and how your skills and talents can contribute to the world.

Recognizing and acknowledging the unique strengths of others is a powerful act of kindness and support. By reminding others of their talents and abilities, we empower them to believe in themselves, pursue their passions, and live a life of purpose and fulfillment.

ᐅᐅᐅ

Connecting, Influencing, And Inspiring Are Lifelong Journeys

Connecting, influencing, and inspiring are lifelong journeys. These 101 strategies offer a roadmap, but the true power lies in your consistent application. Embrace the challenge, experiment, and adapt these strategies to your unique circumstances. Remember, every interaction is an opportunity to grow, learn, and make a positive impact.

Conclusion

As we bring this journey to a close, remember that the power to connect, influence, and inspire lies within each of us. The strategies outlined in this book are not just techniques—they are pathways to meaningful relationships, impactful communication, and transformative leadership. Your ability to implement these will determine your success in making a lasting impression in your personal and professional life. Start small, practice consistently, and watch the ripple effects grow.

Acknowledgments

This book would not have been possible without the encouragement of our readers, the trust of our clients, and the inspiration drawn from countless conversations, sessions, and trainings. A heartfelt thank you to my family, friends, and team at M Square Motivation for their unwavering support. You all inspire me every day to do better and reach higher.

Call to Action

If this book has inspired you, I invite you to take the next step in your growth journey. Join our programs, attend our workshops, or connect with us for personalized coaching. Together, we can unlock your full potential and help you make a remarkable impact. Visit msquaremotivation.com or reach out to us directly at 9542021021. Let's transform your vision into reality.

Resources & Tools

To help you put these strategies into practice, visit the Resources section on our website. You'll find worksheets, templates, and additional reading materials designed to enhance your skills and understanding.

Connect with Me

I would love to hear from you! Share your thoughts, feedback, and success stories:

Website: msquaremotivation.com

Email: info@msquaremotivation.com

Social Media: Follow us on Instagram, LinkedIn, and Facebook for daily inspiration and updates.

Instagram:

https://www.instagram.com/motivation.msquare?igsh=OTJlZnU1NHRqNGJ6

Youtube:

https://www.youtube.com/@msquaremotivations

Thank You Note

Thank you for allowing me to be a part of your journey. I hope this book serves as a stepping stone to a brighter and more impactful future. Keep shining!